SKETCH MAP
NOT TO SCALE

N

KEY

A The House
B Millennium Avenue
C Lake
D Pond
E Lake

1 Golden Gates and Lodges
2 Park House
3 Jubilee Rock
4 White Lodge, Barbrook
5 Caravan Park
6 Cricket Pavilion
7 Ice House and Pond
8 Farm Shop
9 Guidepost
10 Estate Office
11 Millennium Stone
12 Park Cottage
13 Paine's Bridge
14 Queen Mary's Bower
15 Game Larder
16 Stables
17 Farmyard
18 Hunting Tower
19 Sowter Stone
20 Swiss Cottage
21 Calton Houses
22 Russian Cottage
23 Paine's Mill
24 One Arch Bridge
25 Blue Doors Lodge
26 Hob Hurst's House

BASLOW

Heathy Lea

Jumble Coppice

Home Farm

BAR BROOK

Tercentenary Avenue

Dobb Edge

PILSLEY

DUNSA

Handley Lane

Paddocks Wood

EDENSOR

E·R

Maud's Plantation

New Piece Wood

Calton Pastures

A The Garden

C

D
Stand Wood

Old Park (private)

Bunker's Hill Wood

The Warren

Eastmoor

Harland Edge

Calton Hollow

CALTON LEES

RIVER DERWENT

B6012

BEELEY

Round About
CHATSWORTH

Round About CHATSWORTH

THE DOWAGER DUCHESS OF DEVONSHIRE

with photographs by BRIDGET FLEMMING

FRANCES LINCOLN

Frances Lincoln Limited
4 Torriano Mews
Torriano Avenue
London NW5 2RZ
www.franceslincoln.com

Round About Chatsworth
Copyright © Frances Lincoln Limited 2005
Text copyright © The Dowager Duchess
of Devonshire 2005
Photographs copyright © The Trustees of the
Chatsworth Settlement © 2005

First Frances Lincoln edition 2005

A catalogue record for this book is
available from the British Library.

Printed and bound in Italy by Deaprinting

ISBN 0 7112 2537 0

9 8 7 6 5 4 3 2

PAGE 1 Chatsworth – the West Front,
the North Wing and Theatre. The
Hunting Tower is on the hill above.

PREVIOUS PAGE The nose of a British
Limousin cow at Dunsa Farm.

THESE PAGES Details of some of the
endless variety of architectural
decoration at Chatsworth.
Top row: The Hunting Tower, the
stables at Edensor, the cupola of
Paine's Stables; middle row: above
the West Front door, White Lodge at
Barbrook; bottom row: Old English
Lodge, a house in Edensor, the
Russian Cottage.

CONTENTS

Introduction 7

Standing outside the multi-painted barn door of a farm near Chatsworth. The strange mixture of sheds in this redundant farmyard was the inspiration for adding a record of the disappearing agricultural buildings to the library of books and booklets describing this part of Derbyshire. The idea led on to include the architectural curiosities that surround us in this unique and thriving neighbourhood.

INTRODUCTION

The idea for this book came about unwittingly.

A small farm near here, belonging to the Trustees of the Chatsworth Settlement, came 'in hand' after the death of the tenant. It was one among the countless, nationwide stories of an agricultural business that could not provide a living for a new tenant: the acreage and scale of the buildings were too small and did not merit the expense of restoration. Put up in the days when mucking-out was done by a man with a shovel and a wheelbarrow, the farm sheds had doors too narrow for modern machinery, and so had been left to their own devices. Over many years they were patched with anything going – even some cast iron uprights from Paxton's Great Conservatory (built 1836–41 and demolished in 1920) were requisitioned to prop up a lean-to.

While the Trustees decided how the land was to be divided among neighbouring tenants hungry for more land, no maintenance was done and the farmhouse was occupied by a family whose interests were elsewhere. The yard was not a pretty sight, but as I looked at it and the crazy juxtaposition of the buildings, put up higgledy-piggledy, I thought that there were a few architectural curiosities here that should be recorded. So Bridget brought her camera, and photos of the jumble of hay barn, cart shed, cowsheds, pigsties and stables soon arrived.

As more small low-tech farms came vacant the process was repeated. A picture began to emerge of what the farmyards, barns and byres on smallholdings built before the Second World War, when the scale was small, cows had names instead of numbers and horses provided transport and power, had looked like. It seemed to be a Good Idea to record some of them before the inexorable tide of change engulfed the less useful and they were lost for ever.

While we were going round the estate with open eyes, all sorts of other local landmarks, easy to miss because they meld into the surroundings, seemed worthy of note. Of course the House and garden are what people come to see. But Chatsworth is responsible for 450 other human habitations across the 35,000 acres of the Derbyshire estate (12,000 acres embracing Chatsworth, the rest scattered throughout the county), plus an untold number of shelters for cows, sheep, horses, pigs, goats, dogs, chickens, pheasants, plants, cars, tractors, mowing machines, harvested crops and cricket teams. So there are also pigsties, privies, pubs, a pound and a pavilion. Look again and you will see an aqueduct, arches, barns, bridges, bungalows, barrows, byres and a bower; cottages, chapels and churches; drains and a deer barn; gate posts, glasshouses and a game larder; milestones, millstones, mills and a mortuary. There are shearing sheds, sheep dips, steps, stables, stiles, sculptures that are horse trial fences, and a Swiss cottage; troughs, tunnels, weirs, wells, and windows of curious shapes and sizes. It is these that Bridget has photographed and in this album I try to describe.

Whether old or new, grand or humble, beautiful or ugly, these kind of man-made architectural oddities give character to a place and make the English country and its villages what they are. Few pause to absorb them when hurrying in search of their famous neighbour here but they are worth another look at a slower pace, each having had a role in its time. They date from 2000 BC to last week – 4,000 years at a glance – from the purely practical via the improbable to the fantastic, the latter often inspired by the imagination of a Duke of Devonshire.

Hoping to interest walkers and the car-borne, I have included only those curiosities within a couple of miles of the House; and, for the sake of simplicity, I have divided them into four walks that set off from the House in the general direction of the points of the compass. The map explains all. (I must emphasise that the car park at the House is only open with the House and garden. The car parks at Baslow and Calton Lees are always open.) Most of the places illustrated are easily found on the roadside, or on a public footpath or bridlepath. But a few are in gardens or near houses where it would be annoying for the occupants if people were to try to discover them. In these cases the exact place or name is left out for obvious reasons.

As you arrive in the park on the public road and get your first glimpse of the House in its matchless setting – between the woods and the water, as Paddy Leigh Fermor's book – you might think that little has changed over the 450 years since Sir William Cavendish and Bess of Hardwick, the progenitors of the family in Derbyshire, decided to build in this sublime valley.

You would be wrong. The House, garden and surrounding country have been the subjects of revolution as much as evolution. Nothing has remained static. Every two or three generations of Cavendishes have undone or added to what they found. Things have changed, changed and changed again. The steep hill behind the House was once an escarpment of bare rocks, and even the course and the height of the river were altered. Only the hills and the valley themselves have remained as they were.

Less than a hundred years after Bess (1527–1608) died, her house was engulfed by that of her great-great-grandson, William Cavendish, the 1st Duke of Devonshire. The only visible remains of the Elizabethan years are the Hunting Tower on the hill and the much-restored Queen Mary's Bower by the river. Bess's wonderful garden wall, tall and wide, running further north and east than the boundaries of the present garden and punctuated by gazebos, was razed and her fishponds were filled in.

The 1st Duke (1640–1707), served by his architect William Talman and others, as well as by his own architectural instinct, transformed the square block of the house of Bess's building. He employed the Royal gardeners, London and Wise, to lay out a formal garden in the Continental taste – with parterres, terraces, fountains – so suited to the lie of the land and so fitting for the new, classical exterior of the house. The noble Cascade, a greenhouse and Flora's Temple appeared and the Canal was dug. The work was about finished at his death.

Within sixty years these great features had disappeared in a heap of mud. Perhaps it was the architect and instigator of fashion the 3rd Earl of Burlington who persuaded his son-in-law, the 4th Duke of Devonshire (1720–64), that his house should look west instead of east as hitherto. The Duke engaged the much-travelled landscape man Lancelot 'Capability' Brown to extend the park boundary by hundreds of acres to the west to enhance the new outlook. Brown planted the summit of the surrounding hills to give the house a feeling of security which holds to this day.

In this revolutionary plan much of Edensor village and its mill and bridge were demolished and the course of the river was altered. James Paine was employed to build a new bridge, stables and mill. At the same time Brown destroyed the old garden and left its remains beyond recognition. Most of the fountains and ponds were filled in and the terraces were flattened into a vast, sloping lawn. He used all the tricks of the 'romantic' movement, including ha-has (sunk fences) and groups of forest trees on the lawns, to pretend that the garden and park were one – a fashion which caught the imagination of landowners and gave us the English speciality of a park around a grand house and garden.

Two generations later the Bachelor Duke (1790–1858) got to work on his inheritance and built a massive north wing with offices, bedrooms, sculpture gallery, orangery, theatre and belvedere. Together with Joseph Paxton, his head gardener, he made the garden one of the most famous in the world, adding the Emperor Fountain and the lakes on the hill above in order to feed it, the towering rock garden and the Great Conservatory (which spawned the idea for the 1851 Crystal Palace). More than 80,000 people came to see these wonders in the summer of 1849.

Three generations later the Great Conservatory was no more. It was taken down in 1924. Economy, not ostentatious display, was the order of the day in a country that had suffered

A view of the environs of Chatsworth in a hand-coloured engraving after the painting by Thomas Smith of Derby, 1743.

The landscape transformed by the 4th Duke and Lancelot Brown in 1760–64. The Hunting Tower of *c.*1582 is constant.

the appalling depredations of the First World War. The consequences of the Second World War had even more effect. These unprecedented disasters nearly brought about the end of the family's occupation and association with Chatsworth and its land.

Hardly a family in England was left untouched by the two wars, and to single out ours seems invidious; Chatsworth is a drop in the ocean of the larger scheme of things. Nevertheless its existence as an employer in rural Derbyshire as well as a place to visit was of significance to many.

Following the premature death of his father, the 10th Duke, in 1950 and the tragic loss of his older brother, who was killed in action in 1944, it was my husband Andrew's turn to be responsible for it all. He was faced with a punitive bill for death duties at 80 per cent of all he inherited. After a protracted struggle to pay it, he succeeded in his avowed aim to ensure that Chatsworth should remain independent and has handed on a going concern to our son Peregrine (known to us as Stoker). During the fifty-three years of Andrew's tenure much was changed, inside and outside, at Chatsworth, but a balance between adding the new and conserving the old was always kept.

Ideas for change of any kind are no longer limited by what the patron wishes and can afford and the skills of people available to carry out the job. They are now dictated by market forces (see the charts overleaf), or controlled by all the government bodies and quangos that have fingers in the pies of listed properties, whether these be buildings, gardens, parks, woods, roads or rivers.

Now in Edensor, for example, should you wish to make the smallest alteration to the indoors of a house for the comfort of the occupier, let alone outside, you have to understand that the houses are 'individually Listed Buildings in a Conservation Village, within a Grade I Listed Parkland, in an Inheritance Tax Management Plan, in a National Park in UK, Europe'. Approximately twenty-one Authorities or self-appointed pressure groups have a say in what you may or may not do.

Andrew's achievement, supported by a staff of skilful people devoted to the place, has been to steer a course through this maze. With the twenty-first century, taste and interests have leapt into another league. The consolidation of the last fifty years had already begun to include innovation and now the new guiding hands, those of Stoker and his wife Amanda, are full of plans and ideas for the future.

Change itself is a tradition at Chatsworth. There has always been something new to see, something going on. It has never stood still, never been frozen into inaction at any particular time. I think it would be a tragedy if it were made to do so.

The West Front door frames the view across the park to the avenue cut through Paddocks Wood in 2000. Elisabeth Frink's *Barking Dog* stands on the parapet behind me.

This chart shows the change of direction taken by the estate and its trustees between 1955 and 2005. 'Service industries' have supplanted production from timber with a dramatic reduction in the number of employees in the woods from 51 in 1955 to 4 in 2005. The Buildings Department has also been reorganised in the last fifty years and has reduced its number of employees from 42 to 3, with direct labour being replaced by contractors. The Domain men continue to keep the park in order.

The garden and in-hand farms employ fewer men, but the change is not so drastic. The same goes for the Game Department.

The Farm Shop, its Restaurant, catering at the Carriage House Restaurant, retail shops at the House and Stables, and the Farmyard and Adventure Playground and other outlets did not exist in 1955. Neither did the gymnasium, Personnel, Health & Safety, the Sewing Room, Promotion, Education, Marketing and Bookings. These now account for 83.1 per cent of employees.

The staff of the Librarian that was, now Keeper of the Collection, has increased from two in 1955 to four full-time and four part-time now, and Security is greatly increased, on the go twenty-four hours a day.

Department	1955	1990 Full-time	1990 Part-time and Seasonal	2005 Full-time	2005 Part-time and Seasonal
Buildings Department	42	13	1	3	0
Domain	0	6	2	5	1
Forestry	51	12	1	4	0
Garden	27	21	4	22	4
Game & Fisheries	9	8	2	8	1
Farms	18	15	8	14	3
House (including Maintenance, Security, guides, etc)	25	50	63	46	104
Librarian & Art Collection	2	3	3	4	4
Farm Shop & Farm Shop Restaurant	0	17	11	53	54
Orangery & Stables Shops	0	6	12	9	28
Catering	0	3	53	17	89
Farmyard & Adventure Playground	0	2	8	6	10
Estate office	6	17	1	11	22
TOTALS	180	173	169	202	320
	180	**342**		**522**	

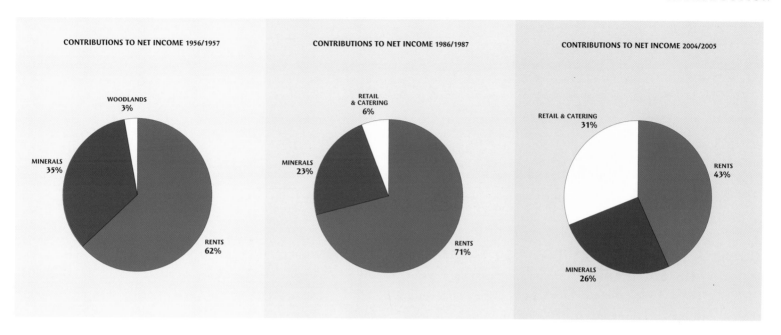

CONTRIBUTIONS TO NET INCOME 1956/1957

WOODLANDS
3%

MINERALS
35%

RENTS
62%

CONTRIBUTIONS TO NET INCOME 1986/1987

RETAIL
& CATERING
6%

MINERALS
23%

RENTS
71%

CONTRIBUTIONS TO NET INCOME 2004/2005

RETAIL & CATERING
31%

RENTS
43%

MINERALS
26%

It can be seen from the chart how the priority of the departments has waxed and waned according to the rise in expectations of our visitors and the gradual eclipse of the traditional workings of an estate. The change over the years is a reflection of that in the country as a whole, where tourism is one of the vital ingredients of national income, replacing the manufacturing output of old.

These pie charts show the proportional changes in the sources of income at Chatsworth over the last half century. In 1956/7 woodlands were still making a net contribution, and in this stony part of the country minerals were responsible for 35 per cent of the income. Thirty years later, the rents from farm tenants and minerals continued to provide the main sources of income, while retail and catering had taken the place of timber. In 2004/5 income from minerals had crept up to 26 per cent, and rents (in spite of many more residential lets), were down to 43 per cent, while retail and catering had leapt to 31 per cent of the whole.

WEST

Walk west from the car park, and you will retrace at least some of the route by which you arrived. This is the most populated of the four routes because it takes in the villages of Edensor and Pilsley, and the hamlet of Dunsa.

QUEEN MARY'S BOWER

In Bess of Hardwick's day there was no parkland to the west of the river. The entrance to Chatsworth was on the east side of the river within the boundary of Edensor, and, bordering the river north of the house, there was a series of fishponds that had been dug to control the ever-present hazard of flooding.

In the middle of what is said to be the last remaining fishpond is a squat square tower, dating from Sir William Cavendish and Bess's day. He was her second husband; her fourth husband, the 6th Earl of Shrewsbury, was appointed guardian of Mary, Queen of Scots by Queen Elizabeth I and in 1570 Lord Shrewsbury brought his prisoner to Chatsworth for the first of several visits. There is a tradition that the unfortunate woman was allowed to 'take the ayre' in the moated building by the river – hence its romantic name, Queen Mary's Bower. It was largely restored by Sir Jeffry Wyatville in 1823–4, but its old bones are plainly visible in the thick walls and broad flight of stone steps over the moat, which make a sheltered place for a picnic. There is nothing inside, and ivy grows on its flat top.

PAINE'S BRIDGE

Walking further west, you cross over the River Derwent by Paine's Bridge, named after its architect. The contributions made by the 4th Duke and James Paine to Chatsworth are of first importance, the stables, the two bridges and the mill in the park being Paine's work. The bridge, 1760–64, replaced one south of the garden. It makes the perfect approach to the House. It is cleverly built at an angle, comfortable to lean on and gaze from,

A winter picture across the West Garden over Paine's Bridge to the park and the estate golf course in the distance.

LEFT A flight of steps over the moat leads to the top of the much-restored Queen Mary's Bower. The water becomes part of one of the fences during the annual Horse Trials, and makes a big splash on landing.

RIGHT ABOVE James Paine's signed drawing for the bridge across the Derwent. Were the stags and river gods a fancy or did they exist? Their plinths are there, but they are not.
RIGHT BELOW The bridge seen from the south.

and the right size and shape for the river as the house is for the valley. It is the place from which to see the golden frames of the West Front windows lit by the setting sun.

Four statues by Caius Gabriel Cibber used to stand on the plinths, two on each side. They must have been commissioned from this Dutch émigré sculptor by the 1st Duke at the same time as other statues for his new garden. In 1958 one on the south side collapsed into the water after a hard frost and two years later a flood caused a north-facing one to fall, so we moved the remaining figure on the north side, St Christopher, to join Neptune on the south side.

It astonishes me to see the heavy loads that pound over the bridge. How could Paine have foreseen twenty-first-century lorries that carry up to 35 tons? But it is regularly monitored and is not found wanting.

MILLENNIUM STONE AND AVENUE

If you fork right and take the footpath to Edensor you will find a big stone set on the brow of the hill to your right, bang in line with the West Front door of the house. Andrew had it put there to mark the Millennium and it is inscribed to tell you so: 'A Millennium celebration to commemorate 2000 years of Christendom'.

It is also central to Millennium Avenue, which we cut in Paddocks Wood at the same time. I had noticed an avenue here on George Unwin's survey of the estate of 1831 and it did not

Looking due west from the Sowter Stone in Stand Wood above the House, Millennium Avenue, cut through Paddocks Wood, can be clearly seen in the distance. Beyond it is a glimpse of the High Peak. The water is channelled from the Ring Pond, which is higher up and further east, to make a waterfall, and thence over the Aqueduct and into the garden.

The Millennium Stone on the brow of the tobogganing hill called The Crobs.

Park Cottage, left in isolation when the rest of Edensor was rebuilt in 1839.

take long to persuade all those concerned that the ha-has in the fields leading up to it were put there not for fun but to carry the eye without interruption to the avenue and the sky.

I am sure there must be more old schemes like this one to be discovered.

EDENSOR

A little further west, running up the hill, is the village of Edensor. It lies within its own enclosure in the park and has the pleasantly secure feeling of a place surrounded by a wall. This was not always so. Till the 1760s the village straggled over the flat ground to the west of the House down to the river. When the 4th Duke engaged Lancelot Brown to make changes to the estate in the 1760s, a mill and some cottages were demolished to make the uninterrupted view we know now. Seventy years later the 6th Duke demolished the rest of the village east of what was the new turnpike road and re-housed the people in his newly built Edensor as it is today.

One house was spared, a little island within its high-walled deer-proof garden. The tenant, Thomas Holmes, was an old man at the time, and the Duke did not wish to disturb him. Park Cottage stands alone there today, envied by passers-by.

The popular notion that the village was knocked down because it was visible from Chatsworth is unproven and, to my mind, unlikely: firstly because it would have been out of character for the 6th Duke, who liked his fellow men, and secondly because the lie of the land meant that only two or three houses would have been seen. The more probable reason was the route of the new road and the park boundary: had the houses remained they would have had to have been individually fenced, thus defeating the object of making that ground into open parkland.

The 14th-century church and some old houses were already there when the work started. Decimus Burton designed a stable block in 1836 with round windows on the upper floor where the stable lads lodged. It now provides eleven flats for single and old people. Then the 6th Duke and Paxton got to work in earnest on the building of Edensor. Out came the *Encyclopaedia of Cottage, Farm and Villa Architecture* of 1839 by John Claudius Loudon, illustrated by his draughtsman John Robertson. The designs in this bible of fanciful and not always practical dwellings give a clue to the origins of many of the architectural features of the houses in Edensor. But I believe the most striking features to have been Paxton's interpretation of the wishes and the taste of the 6th Duke – to the despair of the architectural historian Sir

OPPOSITE LEFT Decimus Burton's stables for Edensor House, 1836, have seen two changes of use. The building was the Estate Office until 1958 and is now eleven flats for single or old people – a most useful role.
OPPOSITE RIGHT The Cavendish family crest is a snake with a duke's coronet above it.

ABOVE The Post Office and Tea Room in Edensor, and the cottage known as Next To The Post Office.
RIGHT The so-called mortuary at Edensor – note the cross in the wall. It is now a store place for the adjacent house.

The 'new' Edensor, mostly built 1839, was executed by Joseph Paxton to please his patron, the Bachelor Duke. Elements of the exaggerated designs in *Sketches from the Picturesque Village of Edensor* by E. Sedding, 1854, are instantly recognisable in a walk round the village. Many of the houses are troublesome to maintain, but the overall impression of Victorian eccentricity is now admired again, after years of derision. High walls hide the less attractive domestic necessities. No pigs were allowed. Vegetables were grown in allotments at the top of the village. There was a communal 'drying ground' below the graveyard wall – no washing line was to be seen elsewhere. It certainly fitted the description of a model village.

Nikolaus Pevsner in the 1960s and to the delight of the present generation, who love the Victorian extravagances.

In a glance you take in a 'Swiss' house, a 'Norman' villa, a one-up one-down cottage hardly bigger than a caravan and an octagonal pavilion. A claim to fame (and a perennial headache for those in charge now) is that no two chimneys are alike. There is a pound, which had a barred window and specially heavy slates on the roof to prevent the escape of inebriates and felons; and a curious building with a large stone cross carved on it, which I have always been told was a mortuary, but no one remembers a body being carried in or out of it. Higher up is another, much older, house and the church.

St Peter's church dominates the village. It is several sizes too big, altogether out of scale, dwarfing and almost threatening the cottages below. It is a product of the deeply religious 7th Duke and the architect Sir George Gilbert Scott, who incorporated some Norman fragments from the previous 14th-century church in his unwieldy new building of 1868. You can see the golden cockerel weathervane glinting over the beeches from Chatsworth. Except for its size, the church is unremarkable till you reach the chapel and the exquisite monument to Bess of Hardwick's sons, Henry Cavendish (died 1616) and William Cavendish, 1st Earl of Devonshire (died 1625). The monument

Edensor seen from The Crobs. St Peter's church, of which the architect was Sir George Gilbert Scott, has dominated the village since 1868.

EDENSOR VILLAGE.

The school, for boys only, was demolished in 1950. On its site, to mourn it, I planted a weeping beech, which now makes a leafy tent for people to sit under.

fills the west wall and is a prime example of the taste of that epoch, when it seems it was impossible to make anything ugly, including the language of the 1662 Prayer Book, mercifully still used in this church.

The marble brothers lie under their grand architectural sepulchre; above them an angel blows a golden trumpet under golden stars set in a marble sky. Henry's empty armour, his helmet with one black feather and one white, and his boots, gloves, gilded spurs and gold-fringed tunic are on one side. William's crimson robes hanging in marble folds with sculpted fur, his sword and earl's coronet, all of Derbyshire alabaster, are on the other. The stony skeleton lying on the mat is, or was, Henry, who was disliked and disinherited by his mother, while William, her favourite to whom she left her fortune, is in his shroud, not yet a skeleton.

This beautiful assemblage of fact and fiction is topped by a broken pediment filled by the Cavendish coat of arms. J. Charles Cox in *Notes on the Churches of Derbyshire* (1877) describes the concoction as 'a good specimen of the costly and heathenish art that adorned the sepulchres of England's great men when the purer taste of medieval had been driven out by the renaissance'. Give me the 'costly and heathenish' when the result is this glorious tomb.

Opposite is the memorial stone to Lord Frederick Cavendish, son of the 7th Duke, Liberal MP for the Northern Division of the West Riding, who was 'sent out as Chief Secretary for Ireland and murdered within twelve hours of his landing in the Phoenix Park, Dublin, May 6 1882 aged 45'. In a glass case hangs the wreath of everlasting flowers sent by Queen Victoria. Such a multitude came to Lord Frederick's funeral at Edensor that the tellers on the gates into the park counted a quarter of a million people. An old woman told Tommy Grafton (forester) in the 1930s, 'That day the throng of men and horses and carriages was such that you could have walked on the heads of the people from Chatsworth to Edensor and never touched the ground.'

The pulpit is supported by stems of Sheldon marble alternating with the rare Duke's Red, both from estate quarries. In a dark corner of an underground passage at Chatsworth lies a heap of Duke's Red. After the fire at Windsor Castle, the architect in charge of the rebuilding in 1997 was looking for some red English marble for the centre of the Garter star on the floor of the new Octagon Room. It was with great satisfaction that Andrew was able to supply this unique commodity for his Sovereign.

Paxton's tomb is bigger than any of the Dukes' and stands in the middle of the churchyard. At the top is the Cavendish family burial ground. Here is the grave of Kathleen Kennedy, Marchioness of Hartington, wife of Andrew's elder and only brother Billy Hartington, and sister of John Fitzgerald Kennedy, President of the United States of America. Billy was killed in action in 1944 and she died in an aeroplane accident in 1948, four years later. A stone slab records the President's visit to his sister's grave in June 1963, a few months before he too met a violent end.

The pair of cottages that flank the cattle grid on the B6019 as you leave the park were designed by Sir Jeffry Wyatville. It is not hard to tell why one is called the Old English Lodge and its mate over the road the Italian Lodge.

THE ESTATE OFFICE

The red-brick building just outside the park has been the Estate Office since 1958. It was built in 1778 by the architect Joseph Pickford as a hotel for the convenience of travellers on the new turnpike road and sightseers to Chatsworth, which has always been open to the public. The bricks were kilned near the

BELOW Sir Jeffry Wyatville's watercolour sketch for 'Cottage Lodges for the Buxton entrance', September 1837.
RIGHT The two houses are unchanged; on the left is the Old English Lodge, its decorative wooden gables all but obscured by wisteria in summer, and on the right is its more severe Italian counterpart. The gate into the park has turned into a cattle grid.

The Grapes Hotel, built in 1778 for visitors to the House, is now the Estate Office.

The same building today; a bunch of stone grapes still hangs in the porch.

Brickhill Pond in the park. The hotel had twelve letting bedrooms and stabling for forty. In 1912 it became the Institute, a club for estate workers, and during that year a big room, now called the Cavendish Hall, designed by architects Sisley and Platt of Manchester, was added and it was used as a convalescent home in the First World War. This room is a blessing to the neighbourhood, serving as a village hall, ballroom, theatre, badminton court, and meeting place for the Women's Institute, the Guides and other clubs; for flower shows, wedding receptions, antiques fairs, plays, concerts, dinners and the annual staff parties. There are now two of these, one for the

permanent and one for the seasonal staff. So many people work here now that they could not all get in at once.

The club has a bar and serves food (there is no pub in Edensor), billiard room, dart board, bowling green and nine-hole golf course. The bar was for men only until 1969 when, to their disgust, the old guard was outvoted and women were allowed to join. In 1975 a tennis court and a large heated indoor swimming pool were added, and in 1999, at Andrew's suggestion, a gymnasium and beauty salon.

Opposite the Estate Office is Teapot Row, which consists of four houses built in 1912 by Cox Wilson, a local builder. It got its

Four houses, built in 1912, comprise Teapot Row.

name from the endless cups of tea drunk by the workmen. It is said that when at last the job was finished their teapot was ceremoniously buried.

DUNSA

If you venture a little further west, you will see a collection of six houses next to some farm buildings. This is the hamlet of Dunsa. The farm buildings are ancient and modern; the latest cow palace was finished in 2004 and is full of contented pedigree Limousins and their progeny. The British Limousin Cattle Society decrees that their names must begin with the letter of the alphabet

denoting the year in which they are born (K, W, X, Y and Z are not used so the list lasts twenty-one years). In a big herd when many names are needed the letter U presents a problem, whereas B is easy. Umbrella, Upsidaisy, Unity, Urich and Umbug (best in a Derbyshire accent) are now a year old.

Dunsa House has a tower, its own ha-ha and a retaining wall which defines its garden and proclaims its lineage. When Andrew and I moved from Ashford to Edensor in 1947 it was occupied by the redoubtable John Maclauchlan, head keeper from 1905 to 1950. Maclauchlan sent for me – there was no question of him coming to my house – and said, 'Lady Hartington, I've sent for you to tell you that you can go wherever you like.' He reminded me of my father and we soon became good friends.

John's daughter, Flora, who was born in 1898, said to me one day, 'You know, we live in a birdcage.' 'A birdcage, Miss Maclauchlan?' I asked. 'Yes. There were several of them, The Rookery at Ashford, Heathy Lea, Calton House and our home, Dunsa House. They were where the 6th Duke kept his lady friends.'

In the case of Dunsa House this romantic idea may not be all it seems. The 6th Duke did, indeed, give it rent free for life to Miss Thornhill when she fell on hard times. She was the daughter of old family friends at nearby Stanton. There is nothing in their correspondence, though, to suggest that they were lovers; rather he seemed to look on her with mild amusement. I cannot discover if she was a fragrant beauty or a bearded old spinster. Instinct tells me she was the latter.

LEFT Dunsa House, one of the Bachelor Duke's 'birdcages' where, according to tradition, he kept a mistress. From 1905 it was the head keeper's house. Since 1952 it has housed various members of staff. The ha-ha dividing it from the field is invisible as intended.

ABOVE A dovecote in the Dunsa Farm buildings. The birds were bred to be eaten, just like any other farm animal.
ABOVE RIGHT A cowshed in one of the sloping fields between Edensor and Dunsa. Before the Second World War, many of the village householders had 'three acres and a cow' and wintered their cows in sheds like this one. It has been restored inside and out to show how it was used in the past.
RIGHT Silage making at Dunsa Farm.

Fields above Edensor, once smallholdings. Several ruined sheds remain.

Eliza Warwick was another matter altogether. She certainly was the Duke's mistress for ten years. He installed her at The Rookery at Ashford in the Water and gave her 22 Dorset Square in London. It seems she was the source of as much anxiety as she was of joy, and their stormy relationship was the subject of many blacked-out passages in his diary.

When Andrew was posted to Italy with his regiment in 1943 I moved into Eliza Warwick's Rookery with a baby, a pony and cart, the usual complement of dogs and a pig. Ignorant in those days of the tenant of a hundred years before, we lived there for four years. (In 1947, Andrew having come out of the army, we moved to Edensor House and stayed there until Chatsworth itself was ready in 1959.)

Of the birds of Heathy Lea and Calton House I know nothing, but their cages are solidly built houses occupied today by less flighty individuals.

The Rookery, Ashford Hall, Churchdale Hall, their surrounding land and nearly all the cottages at Ashford which belonged to the estate were sold to pay death duties in the 1950s. Some of the cottages realised about £50 at the time and it is interesting to see the increase in value when the same cottages are auctioned today.

THE FARM SHOP

The Farm Shop occupies the 9th Duke's Shire horse stud, a lovely range of stone loose boxes with a big hayloft that he had built in 1910 on the outskirts of Pilsley village, a mile and a half from

Chatsworth. It is probably best to go in the car to the Farm Shop to join our regular faithfuls who come from a radius of 30 or 40 miles and seem to like what we provide.

My grandfather-in-law loved his Shires dearly. He attended every foaling, much to the annoyance of his chauffeur, who was often called out in the night to drive him to the stud. Once a mare was foaling when the Duke was in church. He couldn't bear the suspense and walked out in the middle of the sermon, leaving his false teeth in his pew: he always took his teeth out when he was agitated.

We began thinking about a Farm Shop in the early 1970s, when the in-hand farm at Chatsworth was doing very badly. At about that time I became associated with the Royal Smithfield Show, run by a happy triumvirate of farmers, butchers and agricultural machinery makers. Listening to them talking made me want to sell our produce direct to the consumer, thereby helping the farm and cutting out the middle man.

Once we had decided upon the place, we applied for planning permission. As we are in a National Park, this was a slow and strict process, but eventually, in 1976, it was granted. The old harness room, with its welcoming fireplace, was chosen to be the shop. A butcher's cutting room was made in one of the stallion boxes, and we bought equipment to make yoghurt and soft cheese in the dairy. A manager was engaged, and a retired

'Chatsworth Royal Match', one of the 9th Duke's Shire stallions.

The Farm Shop occupies the building that was made to house the 9th Duke's Shire horse stud.

butcher and his assistant. The dairyman who had looked after the Jerseys learned to make yoghurt and cheese, and off we went.

The carcasses were hung in two second-hand refrigerated lorry containers parked against an outside wall, bought because they were cheaper than making a cold room. We ordered thousands of plastic containers decorated with pictures of Chatsworth and Jersey cows for the yoghurts and cream and thought we could sit back and watch the queues of keen customers arrive.

We had not reckoned on the stern realities of retailing food. The requirements of the Weights and Measures inspector are a far cry from a bring-and-buy stall, where the precise quantity in a jar of your delicious home-made marmalade is a hit or miss affair and is accepted as such. Five different inspectors examined our yoghurts and their containers. We had to print such wild statements as '10 fluid ounces, 284 mls liquid, skim milk with added skim milk solids, fruit as per lid, sugar, *Bulgaris lactobacillus, Streptococcus thermophilus'*, which made it sound more like an illness than a health food.

We sold meat only in freezer packs. We made sausages in a second-hand machine, sold game in season including venison, and our Elm Tree arable farm (20 miles away) supplied potatoes and flour milled daily from wheat grown there – the whole grain with nothing added and nothing taken away.

All went well for a time, but difficulties arose, and by the beginning of 1984 there had been four years of escalating losses. The trustees got restive. They said that if the Farm Shop hadn't turned round in two years, it must stop trading. So we had to make radical changes; one was finding a new manager.

We were lucky. Our chef, Jean-Pierre Béraud, passionately wanted to run a shop. He had no retailing experience but a blinkered interest in food and quality, plus a Frenchman's instinct for business. He was appointed manager in 1984 and there was an immediate change in the fortunes of the shop. Having made jam, marmalade, scones and cakes in our own kitchen for the shop, keeping meticulous accounts of every ounce of flour costed, and having understood the demand for cooked food, he made a kitchen next to the shop where pâtés, hams, cakes, biscuits and several kinds of bread were made in a second-hand oven, mixer and steamer, which wafted irresistible smells through the building. This part of the business took off at once and is still growing. British farmhouse cheeses came next, then vegetables, fruit juices, English wine and locally made chocolates. From a loss of £31,000 in 1983 Jean-Pierre pulled the shop round into profit within twelve months.

Still, you can't please everyone. I had two letters from women who had bought a whole lamb for their freezers. Their message was the same: 'When I drive through the park at Chatsworth I see the lambs and they have four legs. When I unpacked the lamb I bought from you it had two legs. What happened to the other two?' They had never heard of a shoulder of lamb.

In 1989, after its rapid growth, the Farm Shop became a department of its own, employing 12 full-time and 6 part-time

Pilsley School in 1950, when Paxton's building of 1849 was unchanged.

The recent additions have left the original building untouched.

staff as well as 8 Saturday juniors and 2 full-time people in the new Coffee Shop at the far end of the building. Now there is a staff of 48 full-time and 52 part-time people.

The shop has an old-fashioned atmosphere, almost like a club: many of the customers know each other, you can park for nothing, the meat is properly hung, you are (I hope) treated politely, and you can find a large selection of food and drink under one roof. The number of customers continues to grow. Many of them use the 90-seat restaurant, opened in 2004. Its windows give a magnificent view over Dunsa.

PILSLEY

The village of Pilsley belongs wholly to the estate: dwellings, school, pub, Farm Shop and post office (which, like the pub, does bed and breakfast). There is a public telephone box, still as red as when they were universal. The village has constructed its own children's playground.

The post-war buildings are the eight Mary Devonshire Cottages (1959) and six bungalows for retired people – the first pair (1950) were a memorial to Billy Hartington, Andrew's elder brother, built of the stone from the demolished school at Edensor, followed by two more pairs in 1970 and 1991.

Memorial cottages for Billy Hartington, 1959. Billy was killed in action in September 1944.

Pilsley school flourishes, but for a time it was a close-run thing. In 1967 when there were only 14 pupils the school was threatened with closure. Now it has 61 children on the roll, and it has been built on to four times: in 1950 (kitchen), 1969, 1998 and 2002, to accommodate ever more and ever younger pupils. Soon they will arrive *in utero*. The Early Years Suite (the swish name for toddlers) for ages 2½–5 years was added in 1998. The estate sends a bus round to collect the children of those who work at Chatsworth. The fact that they all go to the same school seems to strengthen the feeling of 'family'.

In 2004 the Wesleyan chapel in High Street was converted into a computer room for the school. What would John and Charles Wesley say to that? Instead of hymns there is tapping of keyboards. God is sidelined in favour of Mammon to keep up with the Joneses of the 21st century.

The penalty of success of school and Farm Shop is that Pilsley at rush hour is quite tricky now. The escalating number of cars in general has changed the appearance of rural places more than anything else in the last few years. The usual two per house seems fast to be turning into three – a car per bedroom. Added to the native cars are those of walkers and sightseers who are naturally drawn to beautiful places. The village streets are lined with continuous ribbons of shiny metal. Anyone who runs a rural enterprise has the thorny problem of providing a car park: placing it too near the place of pilgrimage will, by its nature, detract from it; too far, and people won't want to walk.

RIGHT Redway Farm in 2005. As you leave Pilsley for Bakewell, Redway Farm is on the left at the bottom of a wooded hill. The motley buildings were thrown up at various times, testaments to many decades of farming diversification – a word so often spoken of now but not always with this end result. Cows, pigs, sheep and poultry came and went according to demand at market. Horses were always there, the only source of power and transport.
TOP LEFT Corrugated iron in the last stages of decay has turned into a thrilling deep ochre-red, thanks to years of rust.
BOTTOM LEFT The cow byre was the winter home of the milkers, tied by chains round their necks for six months of the year and apparently none the worse for it.
TOP CENTRE AND FAR RIGHT Two uprights from Paxton's Great Conservatory of 1841 have a less glamorous role here in propping up a lean-to – examples of improvisation encouraged by economy before the throwaway days arrived.

An example of a well-built Pilsley farmhouse that belied its appearance, as it was in dire need of restoration.

After re-pointing with lime mortar (which will fade) and a re-design of the internal layout in 2003, it now has a new lease of life as a comfortable family home.

Another change that has affected the look of the villages here is the disappearance of allotments. These immaculate plots were such a feature of Edensor, Beeley and Pilsley – they showed the taste in vegetables of the holders, and the produce at the annual village flower show was wonderful to behold. Now they have all merged into a featureless part of a field. At Edensor the hand gates in the wall at the top of the village are the only sign left of the then-necessary vegetable gardens. But some of the best flower gardens in the district are in Pilsley.

In common with other estate housing, changes continually take place in Pilsley. A few are immediately visible, like the enlarged school or previously empty farm buildings that have been incorporated into their attendant farm houses. Some barns and sheds have become workshops: one, surprisingly, contains a brewery; three that have far views across the valley to Baslow and the moors beyond are now occupied by Rory Penrose's upholstery business. There you can find not only the furniture he makes but all the patterns of materials and wallpapers to study at leisure with no fear of Sloane Street traffic wardens. Most of the changes leave outward appearances unaltered; roofs and window frames are renewed but look as if they have always been there.

The majority of alterations come under the heading of repairs and are done indoors: re-wiring, bathrooms made more convenient and kitchens modernised. If the same family has been in a house for upwards of fifty years, which often happens, and then leaves for whatever reason, all sorts of renewals are necessary. The poor design and workmanship of the immediate post-war years, such as a hurried addition of a ground-floor bathroom, laid up a store of expensive difficulties to be dealt with half a century later. Chunks of the building budget are now used to make life more pleasant for the occupants.

Some of the cottages built into the bank of the steep valley that is Edensor were whited sepulchres, unique in their variety from the outside, but damp and dismal inside. They have been made dry and far more comfortable than they were originally.

Improving both the houses for people who work for Chatsworth and those that are let to outsiders is a constant process that is one of the most interesting and rewarding parts of estate management.

OPPOSITE AND THIS PAGE An abandoned farm near Baslow. Planning permission was granted in 2003 to make the dilapidated buildings into a comfortable house. These photographs make it appear an impossible task. It was not a job for the faint-hearted but the satisfaction to be had in bringing these once-sturdy buildings back to life made the effort worthwhile.

A SINISTER ANCIENT MONUMENT

There are several Ancient Monuments around Chatsworth, all protected by reams of paper and official words. One is in the environs of Pilsley. It would be rash of me to tell you the exact place for two reasons. The first is that the Authorities would be down on you like a ton of bricks if you so much as looked at it. You may be inclined to take more notice of the second reason: it has a fearsome reputation for bringing bad luck to anyone who moves it, sits on it or even wishes it was his. Perhaps the people said to be buried under it in the Bronze Age are having their revenge for living at such an awful time.

The official schedule of monuments describes it as 'a bowl barrow surmounted by the base of a medieval wayside cross'. The barrow is a nearly circular mound of earth and stones on the highest point of the farm, next to an ancient right of way. The base of the cross is a hollowed-out stone bowl.

The eighty-year-old daughter of the Pilsley blacksmith told the father of Len Broome, the retired tenant farmer on whose land it lay, that his 19th-century predecessor thought the stone bowl would be just the thing for feeding slops to his pigs. He dug it up, took it to the pigsties and used it for that purpose. All his pigs died. There are more recent instances of bad luck befalling innocent fellows who attempted to use it: they suffered strokes and heart attacks and even their dogs expired for no apparent

The 'cursed' cross base. Look out! KEEP OFF.

reason. Such is its reputation that the officials need not worry about it being stolen or moved. It is as safe as houses.

The 1709 stone guidepost.

THE 1709 GUIDEPOST

Where Edensor Lane and the Handley Lane to Bakewell converge, in the corner of the V-shaped field, stands a 'stoop' or stone guidepost with the date 1709 carved on it and just visible. The directions are shown by a chubby carved hand, three fingers clenched, the forefinger and thumb pointing to 'Bakewell Rode' on one side and 'Sheffield Rode' on the other.

The guidepost is the product of 1697 when Parliament authorised Justices of the Peace to order the erection of guideposts at remote crossroads to direct travellers. Some counties did as they were told immediately, but the Derbyshire Justices dallied for twelve years until 1709, when they were reminded to get on with it forthwith.

This one somehow avoided being destroyed in the Second World War, as so many milestones were for fear that they might help parachuting Germans. Perhaps the local defence people thought the spelling muddling enough.

SOUTH

To discover what lies south of Chatsworth, you can either drive along the B6012, over the cattle grid, and park at Calton Lees, or park at the House, walk over Paine's Bridge and wander for a mile down the west bank of the Derwent.

THE OLD PARK

If you take the watery route, look across the river as you walk, and you will see the Old Park, the only bit of the park at Chatsworth that is private. There, in 190 acres, among the ancient oaks, outliers of Sherwood Forest, the herds of red and fallow deer can find the privacy that they need to rear their calves and fawns. Being too tidy is not always a good idea. Fallen trees have been left undisturbed here since the 1950s, as they are hosts to insects and invertebrates, which in turn are food for the birds. Natural regeneration of the oaks would not work here, as the deer would eat the seedlings, so we harvest acorns from the best trees and grow them on elsewhere for a few years until they are big enough to be planted out, protected by tree guards.

The lower weir on the Derwent. The self-sown alders are brewing up trouble.

The rest of the 1,100 acres of the park – mostly closely cropped grass – and the woods behind the House are yours in which to walk, run, lie down, play games, picnic, sing, shout, be quiet and bring your dogs, children and granny; no one will ask you to go away. Long before National Parks, and the more recent Country Parks, were invented, people have been welcome to wander about Chatsworth Park 365 days a year. The number that come is unknown because entry is free.

I hope people feel they are not bossed about when they come into the park. So many places which pretend to welcome visitors have notices saying 'No Prams', 'No Cameras', 'No Dogs', 'No Games', 'No Picnicking' that I wonder why they don't say 'No People' and have done with it. We beg only that dogs are kept on leads because of the livestock, and that closed gates are closed again when you have gone through them.

Ancient oaks in the Old Park, outliers of Sherwood Forest.

Fallen oaks are left to provide a living for a host of invertebrates.

FARMING AND STOCK

At Chatsworth we raise almost a thousand head of cattle, of which about half are the dairy herd, and half are for beef, plus about five thousand ewes, a number that doubles in the spring when the lambs appear. So two-legged animals often mingle with the four-legged creatures, to the surprise of foreign visitors who are amazed by seeing farm animals grazing right up to the garden wall.

Till 1999 agisted cattle – those that belonged to neighbouring and tenant farmers who needed to save their grass to make hay – summered in the park. Now our own young stock, red-brown British Limousins for beef and black-and-white Friesians for milk, are turned out here from May to November.

For the first few days they beat the bounds in celebration of their new freedom, after a long winter, while the accumulated hanks of muck and hair fall off with their winter coats. They soon become proprietorial and stand about the roads holding up the traffic like a crowd of London demonstrators. Leonard Barnes, chauffeur, used to say every spring as he was hurrying to drive a late-starter to catch a train, 'This is the stupidest lot of cattle we've ever had in the park.'

Managing stock can be a tricky business. Bulls and newly calved cows can't go where people with dogs walk in case anything untoward happens. Added to that, the cattle and sheep have to be moved from the ground where the big park events take place

British Limousins below the garden wall in the Old Park.

Our pedigree herd of British Limousin cattle grows apace. The reputation of the beef, which is sold through the Farm Shop, grows with them. Meat sales lead the shop and beef is the best seller. People see the cows and calves grazing in the park and fields around Pilsley and know they are reared naturally. Some bulls are sold for breeding and we plan a sale of pedigree females and their offspring in alternate years. The white-faced calf (top left) is by a Limousin bull out of a Hereford-Friesian cross heifer.

A Swaledale ewe from the moor and her twin lambs.

Shearing in early June.

while all is set up and until the temporary buildings are taken down some days afterwards. Management is further complicated by the large open area of the park; the 1,100 acres are divided into only three parts.

Before the Second World War, about 2,000 acres were farmed in-hand, and the remaining 10,000 acres around Chatsworth were let to tenant farmers. By 1990 5,000 acres had come in-hand and the figure is much the same today. We also farm 1,000 acres of arable land between Chesterfield and Mansfield.

The galloping speed of change in farming practice in the past fifty years is largely to do with scale and the need for ease of management. Everything is bigger – fields, tractors, sheds, numbers of cows and sheep. The idea is to maximise efficiency and reduce labour costs.

One of the results of this change is the disappearance of many kinds of small birds. People seem to be surprised by the sad fact that the numbers of songbirds, finches, sparrows and starlings are dwindling. It seems to me that you don't have to look very far here to see the reason, which is more or less repeated throughout the country. In the 1950s and '60s six different arable crops – a few acres each of potatoes, oats, barley, wheat, kale, roots (turnips and swedes) – were grown within a mile of Chatsworth.

Shorn ewes, pleased to be rid of their heavy fleeces, and their lambs, on their way back to pasture.

LEFT Stone walls are the age-old dividers of fields and give shelter in bad weather.

ABOVE A lunky hole or smoot is the simplest form of opening in a wall – topped by a single flat stone – that makes an ever-open door for game birds, rabbits and hares. Ewes and lambs, but not cattle or horses, use the larger ones which take the place of gates. They are easily closed by netting or a board. When rabbits were an important source of meat for country people, they were driven into the lunky holes which were netted on the far side to make a trap.

Cattle were out-wintered and so were fed in the fields with hay and straw, leaving all kinds of grass- and other seeds for the small birds. The fodder for the ewes, which lambed in the fields, also benefited the birds.

None of this happens now. The only crop on the 5,000 acres of in-hand farmland at Chatsworth is grass. It is grown for fodder, either as grazing or as silage, in which case it is cut before the grasses, herbs and weeds have had a chance to seed, and fed to the cattle under cover. Silage is of little comfort to small birds. Ground-nesting birds like partridges and larks have no chance of surviving the knives of the silage cutting which coincides with nesting time. On arable farms the fields are ploughed within days of harvesting so there is no stubble to provide insects and seeds over the winter.

Added to the lack of food are the ever-present raptors, protected by law. Sparrow hawks must each kill three small birds a day to survive. What with the buzzards, goshawks, peregrines, hen harriers, ravens (all protected), carrion crows, magpies, stoats, weasels, rats and cats, and the wretched grey squirrels, the reasons for the downward spiral of the population of small birds seem blindingly obvious.

THE DOMAIN

Although the farm manager decides on the number of animals which graze the park, a team of five men, grandly called the Domain Department, is responsible for the day-to-day care of

A grand stile over a deer-proof boundary wall.

The top weir, constructed in the 1760s to alter the height of the river.

trees, roads, drains and litter. The ground would soon degenerate into a dreary expanse of thistles and ragwort were it not 'managed'. To help fertilise the grass, all the muck from the winter cattle yards is spread over the fields and park, and the ground is limed when necessary. Nine miles of boundary fencing, which includes dry stone walls, iron railings and wide ha-has, all formidable enough to contain the athletic deer, must be watched and mended; so must 1,273 tree guards, drains, watercourses, gates, grids, roads and tracks.

There are 7½ miles of private roads in and around the park, 'private' meaning that the estate is responsible for their upkeep, even though people are welcome to walk on most of them. They are tarred and finished with 10mm nominal size Staffordshire pink crushed quartzite gravel chippings, well rolled, which results in a brown colour instead of the navy blue of a main road.

THE RIVER AND FISHERY

If you have taken the water-side path southwards, you may see a rod fisherman pursuing his lonely, but much sought-after sport. There is about a three-year waiting list of prospective members for the Chatsworth Fishery. Over four miles of double-bank fishing, from Baslow to Rowsley, is theirs. Brown and rainbow trout, restocked every year, and grayling provide summer and winter sport respectively. As well as looking after the fish population, the three water bailiffs are responsible for providing

A trout fisherman on one of the most productive stretches of the river.

habitats for many types of wildlife. Control of vermin such as rats and mink is essential, especially when the migratory birds return to nest in the spring.

The two weirs are a reminder that this natural-looking river owes much to the inspiration of a former Duke of Devonshire. The top weir was created in the 1760s, as part of the 'Capability' Brown landscaping. Its purpose was to raise the river level to make it visible from the lower floors of the House and from the West Terrace. It also reflects the House from certain places in the park. Near this weir is one of the few areas of the park where all traces of the medieval ridge and furrow are absent, supporting the theory that massive earth moving was required in the

The day after the gale of 16 February 1962. James Paine's classic mill was mostly destroyed by two full-grown beeches crashing on to the roof.

Paine's Mill today – made safe but not re-built. The stump of one of the offending trees is still there.

landscaping. The lower weir was functional in that it raised the level of the water so that it could be diverted through the new mill to turn the wheel.

PAINE'S MILL

The ruins of this mill of 1756–7 are near the river, not far from the Calton Lees car park. It was working till 1952, grinding corn for animal feedstuffs. Ten years after it closed down two huge beech trees crashed on to it in the mighty gale of 1962, smashing the roof and much else besides.

'Knock it down,' they said. 'Don't knock it down, leave it as a ruin,' said Tony Snowdon, who was staying with us when its fate was being discussed. Leave it we did, and its classic proportions are proof that Paine made sure that a factory can be as pleasing to look at as a palace.

The ruin is a rallying point for walkers and a prime example of the pleasure given to the observer by something man-made in an otherwise 'natural' landscape. Especially if it was drawn by James Paine.

ONE ARCH BRIDGE

At the southern end of the park is One Arch Bridge, the second of James Paine's bridges (1759–60) over the River Derwent, just over a mile downstream from his grand affair in front of Chatsworth. Its parapet is dangerously low by modern standards, hardly hip high, but it has two three-cornered refuges on each side where pedestrians can escape from on-coming cars. It is banned to lorries weighing 7.5 tonnes or more, to the advantage of those who enjoy the park whether they drive or walk. The necessary stop / go lights were some of the first to be installed in such rural surroundings.

The view of Paine's simple and beautiful decoration of the triple-stepped single arch with a projecting dripstone to throw off the rain is blurred by self-sown alders along Beeley Meadow's public footpath. I am too tired to start the lengthy negotiations that would be necessary to allow us to fell these intruders.

Under the bridge a barrier of poles is slung across the river to prevent the deer from swimming out of bounds. There is a similar barrier just above the merging of the Bar Brook with the Derwent between Hare Park Wood and the Home Farm.

THE SPECTRE OF FOOT-AND-MOUTH

During the foot-and-mouth epidemic of the winter of 1967–8 we lived in fear of the deer getting the disease, as it was all around us. The foul-smelling smoke from the cremated carcasses of cattle became horribly familiar. The park was closed to traffic, and with no passing cars there was a strange, almost eerie, feeling of isolation, and one felt that not only the cattle but the human race had succumbed.

On 23 February 2001 the spectre returned to haunt us and a dark cloud settled over the estate. Celebrations like the annual

One Arch Bridge at the south end of the park, designed by James Paine, 1759–60.

staff party, our diamond wedding party and other such gatherings, plus charitable events, were cancelled or postponed. A 700-metre wire fence of the kind builders use was put up to create a 'sterile corridor'.

Anyone who could walk was roped in to herd the deer across the river. The humans were commanded by the head keeper and proceeded as in Grandmother's Footsteps. Slowly, slowly they moved forward; a false move, one deer startled and breaking through the human ranks and the operation would have failed. But they trotted over the shallows near the cricket ground and a second army closed off the area with the portable fencing. Thus the deer were confined to the west of the river and had no human contact.

Disinfectant mats arrived at the entrances to the park, topped up with the violently smelling liquid several times a day. There was no farmstock in the Farmyard. The house opened on 7 April instead of in mid-March. Few people came; they felt guilty about putting the place at risk.

By the beginning of May cash was down £240,000 on admissions, £180,000 on catering and £90,000 on the shops. On 25 May the immediate danger had receded, 90 per cent of the footpaths were re-opened and all restrictions were lifted.

During this worrying time Andrew and the others concerned decided to keep the House and garden open till Christmas in an attempt to recoup some of the spring losses. It was a resounding success – crowds of people came and enjoyed it. No one had seen inside the house after dark before: it was a new world to our regular visitors.

Since then we have kept the House open till Christmas each year, decorating it with lit candles (yes, CANDLES) in all the rooms and providing extra food and drink in the Carriage House Restaurant, with bands and choirs at the weekends for entertainment.

We felt guilty that the direct result of the dead weeks of the threat of foot-and-mouth was this cheerful outcome, compared to the despair of those farmers who lost their stock in such horrible circumstances. But Andrew got letters from hoteliers, owners of bed and breakfasts and many others saying that their trade had also prospered in the dim months of November and December as the result of Chatsworth being open.

CALTON AND CALTON LEES

To reach Calton Lees from Paine's Mill, you cross the B6012 by the cattle grid and take the footpath provided, which leads you past Calton Lees car park. Andrew decided to make it possible for people to park free of charge here, and the car park is much used. Over the years we have planted a lot of trees to hide the shimmering metal on a sunny day, as well as to provide shade for the occupants.

On the left is Chatsworth Garden Centre, built in 1982 by, and let to, John Tarbatt, who started a garden centre in Tansley and

Red deer in early summer. The Old Park is their sanctuary where they are not disturbed by people or cars.

A restored stone water trough and spout in Calton Hollow.

Calton House, one of the Bachelor Duke's 'birdcages'.

wished to expand. He took a lease of 2.4 acres by the car park at Calton Lees for this purpose, and Andrew opened it in May 1983. John is a tenant of the estate, which plays no part in the management but receives a percentage of turnover. The advantage of the arrangement is that it provides income with neither capital investment nor problems of administration, merely the provision of the site. The disadvantage is that there is no control over the merchandise. The Garden Centre thrives.

As soon as you leave this popular place you lose the crowd and pass a pair of cottages built in 1914, the sunniest in the hamlet of Calton Lees, then through the gate and on to a bridlepath along Calton Hollow. The lane winds uphill all the way.

A couple of hundred yards on you pass a stone water trough and its pipes, which have been made to work, and now the water flows into and out of the trough instead of pouring down the road and forming sheet ice after frost. The hanging wood on the right, Cottage Plants, is one of the best pheasant drives of the Chatsworth shoot.

Calton House is a noble building of perfectly proportioned rooms. Evident on a map of 1785, it was enlarged in 1836 and 1855 and the garden was probably bounded between 1831 and 1836 – significant dates when the Bachelor Duke, then in his forties, must have felt the need for women friends. It became one of his 'birdcages', according to Miss Maclauchlan (see page 31). It once

The hamlet of Calton Lees. Once the home of champion Shire horses, it is the end of the road for cars and is visited only by walkers.

had a grand cedar tree that drew attention to its status; that one has gone with the wind now but two replacements were planted in 2005.

By the derelict barn on the right there is a mighty stone trough, a veritable reservoir, and a stone platform, with big paving stones to hold the bank, for the milk churns awaiting collection. No milk now, no collections; like 'Ernie's ghostly gold tops a rattlin' in their crate', it is all change and there are no small dairy farms left, just signs like this one of what used to be.

When the barn collapsed some of the stone slates were recovered intact. They are as big and as neatly cut as gravestones. It is on the list to be rebuilt.

The lane winds round the back of Calton House and in front of its cottage, now nearly hidden by shrubs and climbers in its luxuriant garden, through the gate on to Calton Pastures. There are five Bronze Age bowl barrow burial grounds on these pastures. Dating from 2500 to 1500 BC, they are the usual heaps, fenced against people who are alive, and one promontory fort, which is 'the most important of these ancient monuments – there being only about a hundred in the country'. The fort is regarded as a 'settlement of high status' and is delightfully dated as of the 'later pre-historic period'. These humps and bumps and a mere were the only interruptions to the eye on what was once a

Mortimer's or Clark's Barn at Calton Lees. The holes in such barns are for ventilation to keep the stored hay sweet, but are often used by nesting owls.

276-acre prairie of grass where the High Peak Harriers hunt horses summered and little wild pansies grew. It used to be a pleasure to ride across this open space. Now it is ploughed, re-seeded and divided by dreary wire fences to make possible the harvesting of silage and hay while sheep graze.

RUSSIAN COTTAGE

What a pleasant surprise to arrive on Calton Pastures and see the Russian Cottage in all its originality, a curiosity if ever there was one, a fanciful toy looking west to the sunset. Late in 2004 someone in the House asked, 'Have you seen the doll's house we've found?' I went to look. On the passage by California, a seldom-visited room, is a cupboard that I must have passed a thousand times and so anonymous did it look that I never thought to open it. Lo and behold, inside lay the perfect model of the Russian Cottage, plus a little farm, yard and outbuildings made of Siberian pine, unseen and untouched for probably a hundred years. It was described by the 6th Duke in his *Handbook*: 'The Grand Duke Michel Paulowitch [brother of Tsar Nicolas I] sent me the completest model of a Russian peasant's house, in consequence of inquiries I made, when he came here, as to the method of joining the beams at the corners. It is a chef d'oeuvre of execution and complete finish of all the details, and it is made to detach with wonderful skill and ingenuity.' There is a stove, some Ikea-like furniture, including bunk beds, and standings for horses and cows under its roof. There are still thrilling discoveries to be made in the House.

The view east from Calton House to The Warren.

Follow the bridlepath through the narrow neck of New Piece Wood and another surprise awaits. Choose the afternoon for this journey, open the high gate and with the sun behind you see the whole of the park laid out like a map with the House in its perfect position. The wide view takes in Paddocks Wood to your left, Maud's Plantation of dark Scotch firs, the Farm Shop, the spire of St Peter's church at Edensor and the golf course in the middle view, then over the hills to Froggatt Edge and the Sheffield moors, Chatsworth and its shining greenhouses, Dobb Edge beyond and the Stand Wood bulging over the Old Park.

There are seats where you can eat your sandwiches at leisure, but for years there was a risk – a cross cock pheasant ruled the seats and harrassed people who were looking forward to a peaceful rest. He was a menace with beak and claws till bought off by the best bits out of the rucksack.

Invisible over Maud's is the deep valley running up from Edensor, divided into small fields. Each field had a shed for a cow belonging to the men whose cottages had no place for them. We restored one of them, loft above, hay rack and the standing below. It is now an historic monument.

Go downhill now, along the zig-zagging green carriage drive through New Piece Wood to the B6012, then left for Edensor or straight on to Paine's Bridge and the House.

New Piece Wood was 'new' in the 1760s. A mixture of conifers and hardwoods, it shows 'Capability' Brown's genius for the long view. It was planted in wedge-shaped compartments so that when a section is felled, the line of trees on the horizon remains intact.

The Russian Cottage looks over Calton Pastures. It closely resembles the model (seen far right) sent to Chatsworth by the Grand Duke Michel, brother of the Tsar, at the request of the Bachelor Duke after his visit to Russia.

FORESTRY

The Dukes of Devonshire have always been deeply interested in their woods, treating them with the respect that Britain's only self-generating building material deserves. The woods are an integral part of Chatsworth. There is nothing haphazard about them. In the garden, in the park and beyond, the planting of trees was, and still is, the work of the out-of-doors decorator. Their form, colour, pattern and shape on the contours, and their place in the view, are as important as the arrangement of pictures and furniture is indoors. Like the contents of a room they have to be looked after – however, the difference is that they change and grow. Trees must be planted, weeded, thinned, pruned and, in due course, felled to repeat the cycle.

Most owners of woodland, and all those with a commercial eye on their trees, hope to achieve 'normal forestry'. This is when the acreage of planting equals the acreage of felling of mature trees. The depredations of two world wars, when trees were felled before they were mature, plus the years of neglect between 1926 and 1949, when the woods were not replanted, mean that only 11 per cent of our trees are over sixty years old, whereas 40 per cent should be this age. The history of this sorry state of affairs is not unusual. It happened on other estates in the years of depression and war. 'Normal forestry' here is a pipe dream, which may never be realised.

The outlook for forestry as a business at Chatsworth is bleak. In 1955 51 men worked full-time in the woods. In 1990 there were 12.

Now there are 4. The department is still managed by the Head Forester, but the tree nursery is no more; nor is the saw mill, the tanalising plant, the big tractor with a hydraulic crane for lifting logs or the woods lorry. The work of felling, clearing, weeding and planting is now done by contractors.

In the year to March 2002 the price of standing timber fell by 11.5 per cent in real terms and the following year by another 23.9 per cent as a result of cheaper imports and a flood of timber from the government-run Forestry Commission paid for by you and me, the taxpayers. In 2004 the price rose by 14.1 per cent, but this was an exception and is unlikely to be sustained. The thinnings are almost impossible to sell. The old market for pit props has gone with the pits. Yet if the young woods are not thinned at the right time the final crop will suffer. If the price does not pick up they will have to be 'thinned to waste': unwanted trees will be felled and left for the sake of the quality of those remaining. This unproductive effort would have been unthinkable a few years ago.

The emphasis has had to move from growing timber as a business to beautifying the landscape – a worthy aim, but an expensive one. Government interference and the layers of bureaucracy which concern themselves with the growing of trees seem to belong to world of Alice in Wonderland rather than a steady old Derbyshire estate. After a tortuous procedure of interrogation and lengthy inspections, our woods are now 'certified' (a word that could be wrongly construed).

The south end of the garden is protected by a ha-ha from the Old Park. In the far distance are Paddocks Wood on the right and New Piece Wood on the left of the church spire.

The risky business of felling a dying beech in sections.

Certification means that the estate practises sustainable forestry and works to a plan agreed with the Forestry Commission that felled trees are replaced and all environmental considerations are taken into account for the benefit of future generations. As well as the woods themselves every detail of office management, health and safety, training and equipment is examined, and if you are lucky enough to sell any trees it is a question of 'let's see the bill' to check it.

We are certified under the UK Woodland Assurance Standard (UKWAS), which is approved by the Forestry Stewardship Council (FSC), the umbrella body. There are several certifying agents so, in order to maintain a uniform standard across the industry, the certifying agents themselves have to be certified by the FSC. A charge is made for certification for which there is no return, which adds to the misery of the annual budget, but without certification it is impossible to sell any of our timber, because the sawmills will only deal in timber that is certified. For hundreds of years Chatsworth's woods have done without this circus, but now we must conform. What is the future for forestry? Your guess is as good as mine.

The 'dedication' of woodland until 1989 was an agreement to use the afforested land only for growing trees. This was followed by the Broadleaved Woodland Grant Scheme and the Forestry Grant Scheme. They have been replaced by the Forest Plan in 2000. There have been four different government schemes in eleven years – the blink of an eye in the life of a tree.

In April 2000 a meeting was held here for the latest Forest Plan to be approved by the Forestry Commission. This was attended by them, our Head Forester and representatives from no fewer than twenty-one other organisations which had to be consulted, including the Derbyshire County Council, Bolsover District Council, seven parish councils, the CPRE, Derbyshire Wildlife Trust, Derbyshire Ornithological Society, East Derbyshire Woodlands Project, English Heritage, RSPB and the Ramblers Association.

They met. They talked. They went away to think. In February 2001, only ten months after the meeting, they let us know that they had agreed and that we could proceed with our twenty-year plan.

Part of the negotiations involved bowing to green pressure groups who wanted some plots to be left to 'natural regeneration' after felling. If, after five years, such a scheme is deemed to have failed, the area can be replanted with the help of a grant. You do not have to be a clairvoyant to know that a few sycamore suckers will grow from the old stumps and that's about it. Five wasted years and an impenetrable jungle of briars and rhododendrons make the task of clearing the area ready for planting once more an expensive one.

The industry is on its knees – no one in the chain of growers, forestry contractors, timber merchants, sawmills and processors is making a decent income from timber production at the moment.

The old way of felling in *c.* 1900 – manpower with no mechanical help.

In spite of all this gloom regarding the business aspect (which is probably unknown to most of our visitors), there is intense pleasure to be found in the woods and the park trees at all times of the year.

BLUE DOORS LODGE

Once back in Calton Lees, cross the One Arch Bridge and walk a little further east and you will see the Tudor-style lodge of 1835 at the south (Beeley) end of the park called Blue Doors Lodge. Why Blue Doors? I don't know. It once had an important role as it was used by travellers by train to Rowsley, the nearest station to Chatsworth. Rowsley, just south of Beeley, was the destination of visitors, both Royal and those on Thomas Cook's original packages. Its listed ticket office and waiting room still stand, isolated reminders of another age, now dwarfed by modern commercial buildings. Kings and coals entered the park through the two gates at Blue Doors. Royal carriages swept through the grand one in front, and the carts carrying the endless supply of coal needed for the House and the Great Conservatory used the humbler affair round the back.

The road through the Old Park is closed to traffic now except on days of big events.

BEELEY

Go back to One Arch Bridge, climb the stile on your left and have a pleasant walk over Beeley Meadow to Beeley village. Some of

The Blue Doors Lodge at the south end of the park.

the most interesting houses on the estate are here. Two are early 17th-century: Norman House (called after the family who owned it for hundreds of years, not built by the 11th-century invaders, as passers-by are sometimes heard to suggest) and Beeley Old Hall. The bedrooms on the first floor of this grand old house are divided by single panels of wood, so the private noises of snoring and cleaning of teeth are public. It has a dry-stone garden wall of remarkable construction strangely reminiscent of those built by the Incas on the other side of the world at about the same time.

The Duke's Barn (1791) once did duty housing livestock and crops from land belonging to the Old Hall. It was leased for

The Parthenon on Bridge Farm near Beeley.

The Duke's Barn was remodelled in 1791, and again in 1986 for the Derby Royal School for the Deaf.

nothing by Andrew to the Derby Royal School for the Deaf in 1986 and it is used by them and by other city children to see for themselves what goes on in the country. Paxton built the school (1841), which is now two small bungalows for single people, next to it. Pig Lane was the old road to Chatsworth. The sties have been oddly truncated – no room for a pig now.

West of the river is a singular building, an oddly constructed barn, belonging to Bridge Farm. Somehow it was christened the Parthenon, a name which has stuck and no doubt will soon appear on a serious map. Barn owls nest in it, and in 2005 several young ones were successfully reared here.

In the grandly named Devonshire Square there are three houses built in 1856 by G.H. Stokes, their heavily leaded diamond-paned windows so pretty to look at from the outside yet making it so sadly dark inside.

There is a stream, a pub and a church. Some bollards of monstrous proportions and out of scale with the inoffensive little stream appeared in 1988. What their purpose is I cannot imagine.

EAST

Wherever you go to the east of the House involves a climb uphill. From the Farmyard, go onwards and upwards to reach the lakes that drain the moor to feed the waterworks in the garden. But first see James Paine's Stables of the 1760s, commissioned by the 4th Duke and surely the best 'improvement' imaginable.

THE STABLES

It is worth stopping to stare at this horses' palace, with its vast rusticated stones – 'Cyclopean rustication on the columns; gaiters indeed for a giant', as Alec Clifton-Taylor described them – and tall arches under coved plaster ceilings that made a covered ride for winter exercise inside the stable yard. There were stalls for 80 horses (including carthorses) and a blacksmith's shop. A fountain in the middle provided fresh water. It must be one of the most beautiful buildings in the country and deserves a long, long satisfying gaze from every angle. Reminiscent of a Roman palazzo, it underlines the importance of the horse to the grandees of the time. Two ranges of loose boxes and stalls remain untouched, but the rest is throbbing with life.

On three sides of the quadrangle, above the stalls and loose boxes, there are now flats where stable staff were once housed. 'Third Postillion' is still painted on an office door. The fourth side is the granary, where fodder for the horses was kept. The granary is now a store for mouldings, frames and fittings from Devonshire House, Piccadilly (sold in 1920 and demolished in 1924), the skeletal remains of domes from four-poster beds (thrown out by Evelyn Duchess because she thought they induced sore throats), painted pelmet boards and a thousand other dusty curiosities. All these are sheltered by three-quarters of an acre of roofs. The Carriage House, now a restaurant, was added by the 6th Duke in the 1830s.

The arms in the pediment over the west entrance to the stables were carved by Henry Watson in 1765. The stags' horns

BELOW The old covered ride. After years of desertion and littered with old cars, this part of the stableyard is now busy all through the season providing food and drink for our visitors in beautiful surroundings.
RIGHT ABOVE The stable staff in *c*. 1900. Some of the men lodged in the rooms above the stables. Some travelled with the family to London and the Duke's other houses by special train, taking the horses and all their paraphernalia with them.
RIGHT BELOW A postillion landau drawn by four horses, *c*. 1900.

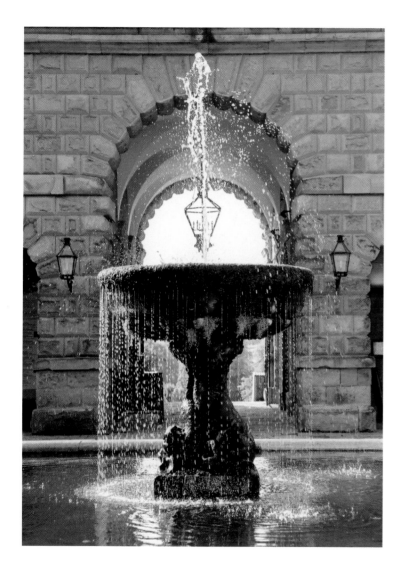

are real. Henry also laid the black-and-white marble floor in the Painted Hall in 1779. He was another talented member of the local Watson tribe, which included his grandfather, Samuel, whose superb carvings at Chatsworth, in wood and stone, rival those of Grinling Gibbons.

THE GAME LARDER

Before you begin the uphill walk, you may catch sight of the little shell of a building in the trees. It is, or was, the Game Larder. It was constructed in 1910 to hang 4,000 pheasants. In Edwardian days of exaggerated entertainments for weary grandees who expected, and received, the best of everything, bags of pheasants at Chatsworth were enormous. The set-piece shoots at which King Edward VII was often a guest were on a grand scale and the game books record the numbers. Anything less than 1,000 head killed in a day was unremarkable.

A prodigious number of rabbits and hares were also shot. Before myxomatosis destroyed most of the rabbits in the 1960s, the fields bordering the woods were grey with them moving unwillingly to cover when disturbed. Thankfully there are very few now.

OPPOSITE Lodge Hill, the steep drive to the Stables. The clock with gilded hands and numerals is wound twice a week. It is a tricky job, assigned to someone who becomes expert at it. The walnut avenue was planted in 1948. Sadly the trees now obscure the Stables and will surely have to go.

LEFT Continuous fresh water, provided by the lakes on the hill above the Stables, feeds the fountain in the stableyard.

The windows of this giant larder were filled with zinc punched with holes to allow the circulation of air to keep pheasants and other game fresh. Larders made of a wooden frame, similarly zinc-windowed, were hung on the north wall of every cottage till refrigerators arrived. We found the plans of this building a few years ago and they show a domed roof.

Here I keep hens, up to 250 of them, the free-est range known to poultry. I like to think it is the only listed hen house in the country.

The floor is covered with straw or shavings, cleaned out every so often when the hens, roosting on their perches above, have added a few inches of precious manure. Under all this is a wonderfully decorative floor of swirling green and mauve mosaics, tough enough to survive the scraping of a shovel when the place is being mucked out and seemingly as bright as the day it was laid down. An unexpected floor for a game larder or for a hen house for that matter.

A few years ago a fox killed a number of layers in broad daylight. There were feathers everywhere and the headless mangled birds were a sorry sight. The corpses were photographed and photos are displayed in the Farmyard to show people the destructive ways of foxes, often thought of as a species of wildlife that must be preserved at all costs.

ABOVE AND OPPOSITE The Game Larder, built in 1910 to hang pheasants, is now a home to poultry. It is conveniently near the car park so they can join in picnics. Among my free-range hens are White Leghorns and Welsummers.

Nineteen bowler-hatted or capped gamekeepers in the 1930s. On the seat in a trilby is John Maclauchlan, the formidable head keeper who ruled with a rod of iron from 1905 to 1950.

GAME

Most of the shooting at Chatsworth is now let to a syndicate of long standing. We invite our friends on the few days we keep for ourselves.

It is difficult to define the reason a day's shooting can be so enjoyable, and no doubt everyone who does it has his or her own ideas. For myself, I love the country in the winter when every detail of the near view is visible, and a short hour of sunshine reveals unsuspected brilliance of colour in bark, moss, rock and bracken, while the long view of trees and hedges is unencumbered by the blur of leaves. There is a purity in the grey and brown of the distant naked landscape, unknown in summer.

I like the endurance test, the uncertainty and endless variety of the weather, the days of cold and wet and merciless wind which turns what was once your face into a featureless lump of porridge, and the mild damp days when insects fill the November air.

The dogs are part of the pleasure. No worker has more enthusiasm for his job than a shooting dog, and if you have one of your own its performance takes on an importance that far outweighs the number of birds it finds. The little triumphs which only the owner notices are intensely satisfying and make up for all the bad behaviour which everyone notices.

The loved old dog watches a drive with fervent interest and anticipates everything that happens. When it is over he knows the likely places to search and stays as long as he, not you, may think necessary; he hunts the familiar ground and usually comes back carrying something. The rusty look and the short stiff stride of the canter of an old dog overtaken by a fresh young one with shining coat and eye are sharp illustrations of the difference between age and youth, and as a dog's working life is only a few years the cycle repeats itself with alarming speed.

My father-in-law did not approve of women shooting, so I never fired a gun till after he died. I was already thirty. At that time (1950) most owners of shoots shared his view and few women shot. After I had been practising at home for a year or two some kind friends invited me away to shoot, and I noticed

A 'gun' and his loader at their 'peg', waiting for the 'drive' to begin.

Heather burning on Eastmoor. Some of the old heather is burnt every year to encourage new growth, food for the grouse.

how wary the other guns were of a female in the line. It was as if some unwritten rule had been broken and a frightful and unnecessary risk was being run. After a while I seemed to be accepted, and when I was shown into the gentlemen's lavatory at Welbeck I knew I was considered to be a real gun at last.

Keepering is lonely work of long hours, no weekends, few days off and short holidays; a calling more than a profession. We get many letters from boys wanting to be keepers, but I wonder if they realise what it entails.

Today there are four gamekeepers and one trainee, and three river keepers. They are the eyes and the ears of the remotest places on the estate. Their hours of work are not fixed and you are as likely to meet them in the middle of the night as in the middle of the day. They know where the badger setts are and prevent badger diggers from indulging in their vile 'sport'. They carry out controlled heather burning on the moor, essential to encourage fresh young growth for the grouse to feed on, they build and maintain the butts on the moor and generally act as wardens over the park and its environs, but their chief concerns are the birds and the fish.

High in importance of their duties is the control of vermin, to allow grouse, pheasants, partridges and ducks to nest and bring

Dogs can be left safely in the shade, where bowls of water are provided, while their owners visit the Farmyard or Playground.

up their young without murderous onslaughts by rats, stoats, weasels, grey squirrels, carrion crows, jays, magpies and other carnivorous predators. The collective term 'vermin' to describe these creatures seems to have gone out since Aneurin Bevan's speech of 4 July 1948, when he described all Conservatives as being lower than vermin. Now these creatures have been promoted to Wildlife and star in television films nightly.

It goes without saying that where the vermin are kept under control there are far more songbirds, and the reason is easy to see. Their enemies are the enemies of the game birds, and therefore of the keepers. Anyone who has watched a pair of

magpies rob a small bird's nest will have been sickened by the sight. Like foxes, magpies have invaded the outskirts, and even the inskirts, of towns and cities.

There are two herds of deer in the park: about 75 red deer hinds and stags, and 225 fallow deer, does and bucks. They are looked after jointly by the Game Department and the Farms. The culls, mostly surplus young males, are sold as venison through the Farm Shop, where the demand outstrips the supply. A few hinds are sold live for breeding to deer farmers.

THE FARMYARD

The Farmyard started in 1973 in response to many letters we got when The Environment was invented and muck and mud were suddenly of interest. Teachers wanted their pupils to see farms and forests, and learn how the land is used, and why and how we keep cows and sheep.

Having decided upon the site, a cluster of buildings which was the old Building Yard, we gathered typical examples of the commercial stock of this district and fenced some paddocks. Some rare breed pigs were added for general interest. A deep-litter house was made for hens, with nesting boxes at an angle so that people could see the eggs being laid. The children also have the opportunity to see chicks hatching every nine days in a see-through incubator.

A litter of Large White piglets under their lamp in the Farmyard.

Two goats are milked in front of a crowd of incredulous children every morning – but the highlight of the day is at 3.30 p.m. when there is a demonstration of cow-milking with a commentary. We wanted it to be as real as possible, with modern machinery. There is only room for three cows (Friesian, Jersey and Shorthorn) so Fulwoods, makers of milking machines, were astonished when we asked for a system to milk one cow at a time. To their credit they produced it, plus a little cooling machine, all arranged sideways on, so that the crowd, gathered on staged wooden steps, can see what is happening.

Milking is followed immediately by the bucket feeding of the dairy calves, which are housed close to the suckler cow and calf so that the different ways beef and dairy stock are reared can be explained.

Watching the children watching the milking is fascinating. They remain transfixed until moved on by teachers or parents. They listen to what is said, and then come the questions – or comments. One little boy from the middle of Sheffield said, 'It's the most disgustin' thing I've ever seen in me life. I'm never going to drink milk again.' Another shot up his hand and said, 'Please, Mister, our milk doesn't come like that.' It's a lesson to the grown-ups to realise how little the children know and how much they would love to know.

It is sad that, because of the rules, the children can't have a taste of the milk after the performance. They are so amazed by the whole thing that I'm sure they think that the milk is not real, and certainly not drinkable.

In 1986 we added a trout-rearing exhibit in two fibreglass tanks with constant running water from a stream off the hill. The fish are bought as fingerlings and grow on here for two years, producing 1,000–2,000 rainbow trout weighing three-quarters of a pound, which are then used to stock the river. Fish pellets are sold at the entrance kiosk and children love feeding them and making the water boil with jumping trout.

I would dearly love to get the children nearer to the animals so that they could touch them, smell them, feed them and try milking the goats, but up to a thousand people go through the place in a day at the height of the school outing season in May, June and July, so the poor creatures would be hugged, patted and milked to death. However, we have introduced three sessions each day when children can handle guinea pigs, goat kids and lambs (watched by staff members). A lot of handicapped children come, and their joy at seeing the animals makes me wish we could do more to get them closer together.

The Oak Barn was added in 2004 to give cover to the children in our uncertain climate. The bones of it are the uprights and beams used to build a 'farm shop' at the Royal Show in 1995, where it won first prize. This and the Education Room have audio-visual equipment for talks and demonstrations. There are also special 'themed' weeks throughout the year, when rural skills, such as dry-stone walling, spinning and bee keeping, or farming occurences like lambing or shearing, are shown. All are hands-on and, when possible, the visitors take home what they have made.

In 1983 an Adventure Playground was added higher up in the wood, and in 1998 the original equipment was replaced with water play, mini-diggers, a trampoline and high towers – an immediate success. Children love toying with the sensation of fear, and there they can happily indulge in just that. The ground is covered with wood peelings, which make good stuff to fall on.

July 2003 saw the thirtieth anniversary of the Farmyard and the launch of a 28-seater trailer, custom-built to satisfy Health & Safety standards, pulled by a big tractor. This has opened up areas of the estate to people who can't walk far. The trailer tours go into Stand Wood and a commentary covers the history of the wood, the lakes and waterfalls. It is very popular, but not many trips take place without at least one passenger being lulled to sleep. The schools use this trailer as well, and enjoy a ride through the north park to learn about the management of the parkland and the animals that graze there in the changing seasons. The sight of the herds of red and fallow deer thrills them. However, the smaller children like the 'bumpy road' and the fact that they are being towed by a big blue tractor more than anything else.

In 2002 the Farmyard remained open until Christmas for the first time. When it gets dark early, the things to see and do have to change and when the weather is bad there is a need for indoor activities. There are still animals to see, but the dairy cows return to our main farm. Daily craft sessions are given, with lots of glue and glitter, and weekends include the much-loved Nativity plays,

Children riveted by a milking display at the Farmyard.

when the children act the story of the birth of Christ, dressed for their parts with the clothes provided, accompanied by a real donkey and sheep.

We can only scratch the surface of the deep chasm between town and country; nevertheless I believe the Farmyard is of value in that it explains the basic facts about the production of milk, meat, wool and eggs and describes the life cycles of the stock, and how they are fed and looked after. It shows that the most ordinary farm animals are as interesting as lions and tigers, and that even grass and trees, taken for granted by people who are not directly responsible for them, are crops to be harvested.

STAND WOOD AND THE HUNTING TOWER

The way into Stand Wood is over the cattle grid in the road or through the gate above the Stables. There is no entrance to it from the garden.

Until the 18th century this was a rocky escarpment devoid of trees. By 1772 the wood was part of the 4th Duke's Pleasure

To walk through Stand Wood is a pleasure at all times of year. There is a great diversity of species and trees of all ages, which makes it interesting whichever road you choose. A few old beeches, miraculously untouched in the 1962 gale, are grand specimens. Hollies and yews regenerate naturally and make a change of colour in the winter. There are rocks and ponds, and some wonderful views.

OPPOSITE A snowy Hunting Tower seen from below the Farmyard.

LEFT The view from one of the windows in the Tower. The House and garden below look like toys and the far view is far indeed. It can be an exciting experience to stay here in winter when the Tower is battered by rain and wind till you feel it is swaying with the trees. In spring the dawn chorus wakes you with a tremendous row and the sunsets are memorable.

ABOVE Part of the stone-slated shed in the dark trees behind the Tower was its wash house (the boiler and stone sink are still there); a couple of pigs lived in the other end.

The Tower must have been a difficult place to bring up a family – miles from a shop, only one room on each floor and precipitous winding stone stairs that are impossible for toddlers, yet I remember a couple with children who were apparently content to be there. The mod cons installed inside now would astonish them.

Grounds, laid out by the Duke and 'Capability' Brown, with paths for walks through the trees planted in the 1760s. Between 1835 and 1845, Paxton created more walks and carriage drives for the 6th Duke. The rocky hillside remains criss-crossed by footpaths and flights of steps, kept in order for your pleasure by the Domain men.

From antiquity a 'stand' has meant a place at a height for spectators, and Stand Tower is the old name for the building from which the wood took its name; Hunting Tower is a later, romantic name. There are two ways of reaching it: either you can climb the perilously steep flight of stone steps or you can walk the easier, duller way, along the winding tarred road. Built in about 1582 at the north-east corner of the park wall of Bess of Hardwick's house, it has a commanding position overlooking the House with huge views to the north, west and south that suggest a guardian role in that uneasy time when many houses were still fortified, but historians tell us it was a pleasure dome from where Bess could watch the hounds working in the valley below.

The Tower survives intact and unaltered outside. There is one room on each floor, the walls are 3 feet thick, and a spiral stone stair occupies one of the turrets from cellar to roof. The turrets have elaborate plasterwork ceilings, perhaps by Smythson who worked at Hardwick Hall, Bess's architectural masterpiece, 17 miles away. In one of them the floor is thick with dead bees. The iron cannon came from a ship which fought at Trafalgar; they were last fired at a celebration here in 1926.

The tower is now a holiday place where people can stay. We have added another bedroom by converting what was the wash house and pig sty. It is remote enough to give a feeling of isolation and people seem to like it.

When you have had your fill of the view from the Tower, go back to the main track and turn right to walk past the Emperor and Swiss Lakes, and the Ring Pond if you can find it, the three lakes on the 'shelf' above the House, which are fed by springs and man-made conduits that cross the moor. These normally carry 3,000 gallons a minute, but at times of heavy rain, 50,000 gallons a minute may have to be 'run off' with a system of shuttles (doors) to turn the water safely into the river. Sources of the watery embellishments that bring life, sound and movement, and sometimes surprise, to the garden, the lakes have a much wider influence than a mere list implies. Without them, there would be no Cascade, no Emperor Fountain, no Sea Horse Fountain or Stableyard fountain, no Aqueduct and no Revelation. Nor would there be electricity in the House, or high-pressure fire hydrants (though both can be supplied by alternative sources).

Two springs in Stand Wood, which were probably one of the reasons that Chatsworth was built here, could supply enough sweet water to meet the demands of up to two million visitors each year. Even the needs of half a million require prodigious quantities. On an average summer's day when around 3,000 people come and the restaurant is going full blast, about 18,000 gallons are used by taps and lavatories.

The Emperor Lake, named after the Tsar of Russia, was dug in 1844 as a reservoir to feed the famous fountain of the same name.

EMPEROR LAKE

The first lake you will see was named after the Emperor of Russia. It was dug to create that great jet of water in the Canal, the Emperor Fountain. Having visited Russia and seen the fountain at Peterhof, the 6th Duke was determined to have an even higher gravity-fed fountain at Chatsworth to impress, and honour, the Tsar on his proposed visit in 1844.

In December 1843 Paxton began his survey and the different levels were taken. A 2½-mile conduit, later called the Emperor Stream, was dug across the moor high above Chatsworth to drain the spongy peat into a new reservoir, the Emperor Lake. Digging the lake was a colossal enterprise, involving the removal of about 100,000 cubic yards of soil by shovel, wheelbarrow and horse and cart, and the building of a masonry dam: 'I walked up with Paxton to see the new reservoir, half frightened by the immense work,' the Duke confided to his diary. However, the 9-acre reservoir was duly completed without mishap, with an average depth of 7 feet and at its greatest, a depth of 13 feet. It was equipped with a drop valve, a waste pipe and a valve for overflow.

The supply to the fountain was described in Paxton's *Magazine of Botany* of 1844, which he dedicated to the Tsar: 'Much consideration was given to the nature of the pipes which were to convey the water … to the fountain, in order that, while security and strength might be obtained on the one hand, no unnecessary waste of metal might be occasioned on the other.' The chosen pipe, exactly half a mile long, was of 15-inch bore and a maximum of 1½ inches thick. Its joints were turned and bored, with clip sockets for additional security. The total fall of the conduit was 381 feet, including 200 feet at 1 in 2. It was necessary to cut a trench out of solid rock 15 feet deep in places, and two ponds had to be crossed. Near the fountain was a double-acting valve, which took five minutes to open or close fully, so that shock damage to the pipe could be avoided. The nozzles of the jet were made of brass: the normal jet would play 267 feet and is on record as having reached 296 feet.

ABOVE The Ring Pond is another reservoir, dug in the 1820s. It is hidden away from the road and made a good swimming pool before people got fussy about clean water.

The work progressed at great speed in the winter of 1843–4, going on all night by the light of flares, and it was ready on time – only six months after it was begun. Alas, the Tsar did not come to Chatsworth but it was called the Emperor Fountain in his honour. It is a rare sight to this day, still the highest gravity-fed fountain in the world.

RING POND

Close to the Emperor Lake is the Ring Pond, another, smaller artificial reservoir for the garden waterworks, constructed between 1824 and 1831. It used to be our bathing place. It even had a diving board, which has long since disappeared. There was something therapeutic about swimming slowly among the ducks and moorhens on a rare hot day. If you swallowed a mouthful of water it went some way to fulfilling my mother's dictum that you should eat a peck of dirt a year.

SWISS LAKE AND COTTAGE

Further east is the Swiss Lake, which was dug in the last years of the 17th century to supply the Cascade for the 1st Duke. It was referred to as the Reservoir until 1839, when the Bachelor Duke returned from a journey to the Continent, where he was

The smoke from the furnaces that heated the Great Conservatory of 1841 was conducted underground through the garden and emerged 265 yards away through this chimney over the wall in Stand Wood. Over 300 tons of coal and coke were consumed by the great stoves each winter, so this long flue ensured that the garden was free from smoke. Paxton's genius at work.

delighted by all things Swiss. He built the eye-catching cottage with its elaborate gables, across the water and gave both lake and cottage their Helvetian titles.

THE SOWTER STONE AND THE AQUEDUCT

The Sowter Stone (no one knows the origin of the name) is one of the many boulders on this high track. Paxton must have

LEFT Looking north-west over Swiss Lake, from behind Swiss Cottage with the Norway spruce of Bunker's Hill Wood in the foreground. The lake, dug in the late 17th century to hold water to supply the 1st Duke's Cascade, was renamed by the 6th Duke.

ABOVE LEFT AND RIGHT Swiss Cottage, built in the early 1840s and one of the most isolated houses on the estate, was one of the 6th Duke's fancies.

noticed its unrivalled position, from where you can look down to the House below, over the park to Edensor and its big church, and up the avenue through Paddocks Wood several miles to the High Peak beyond

The stone is like a saucer holding water which flows into it from the Ring Pond, partly through a ditch and partly underground. The water tumbles over the edge of the rock, down the rift to reach the Aqueduct below.

The Aqueduct is another of Paxton's creations for the 6th Duke, built purely for the pleasure of looking at it. 'The idea', wrote the Duke in his *Handbook*, came from 'one on a gigantic scale' that he had seen in Germany. But he confessed: 'Had I to

Water from the Ring Pond drips over the Sowter Stone.

It is channelled to the Aqueduct – a dangerous path to walk.

The Aqueduct's tall arches are blurred by trees and vegetation.

Water flows into a rocky stream and under the road to feed the Cascade Pond.

build it again, it should not be true, as now, to the cascade, but, by taking a slanting direction, should show its arches to the West; for nothing can be more beautiful than the icicles formed by the dripping from those arches in fantastical shapes during the winter.' It is built of enormous hunks of rough stone. These are invisibly cemented inside the uprights, giving the impression of a dry-stone edifice.

THE WARREN AND HOB HURST'S HOUSE

Leave Stand Wood at the southern end, with Park Farm on your left, climb a high stile over the boundary wall and you will find yourself on The Warren. Look west across Beeley and the Derwent Valley for a stunning view which stays with you for 1¼ miles to the next stile. For Hob Hurst's House, take the first track to the left on The Warren. This rises about 150 feet round the south end of Bunker's Hill Wood.

A different approach is to walk across Eastmoor from the A619 (from the Baslow side of the Robin Hood Inn) which will bring you to the top of Harland Edge, 1,100 feet above sea level. Hob Hurst's House is another Ancient Monument. Going in search of this highly undesirable residence you walk along a track through the heather accompanied by linnets and other little birds belonging to the moor. Usually there is a keen wind

A Swaledale ewe and lambs on The Warren in late summer. The far view over the park and woods reaches the boundary between the Chatsworth and Haddon estates.

A cross base near the footpath which crosses The Warren.

blowing, which penetrates the thickest coat sold at a stall at our Country Fair. On a rare, still day it is a lonely paradise uninterrupted by noise or ugliness or man-made bothers. You are lulled into thinking few have passed that way, it is as nature intended and you are an explorer wondering why Hob Hurst chose to build his house in such an unlikely place.

Then, smack, bang, there is a notice. It tells you, in capital letters, what you already knew unless you are a complete moron: that you are in OPEN COUNTRY. It goes on to warn that you are in an ecologically sensitive area and that you must not cause disturbance to vegetation and wildlife. The illusion of loneliness is destroyed and back you come to the atmosphere of

The notice proclaiming 'OPEN COUNTRY' on Harland Edge.

Among the heather and bracken near Hob Hurst's House.

the hot office where it was written, to stultifying officialdom and all that goes with it.

If you have the spirit to continue, you walk on tiptoe in case of damaging the ecology or anything else. You know you have reached your goal when another notice looms, this time announcing that Hob Hurst's House is managed by the Peak District National Park Authority in co-operation with English Heritage. It warns you that Hob Hurst's House and its environs may be dangerous for children, who must be kept under control.

So you look in vain to see where the danger lies. This protected 'house' is just a little mound, as anonymous as many others on the moor. It is described as 'a square, banked and ditched burial cairn with cist'. It is the grave of Bronze Age people, who seemed to like being buried on high ground. Who Hob Hurst was I do not know and why he chose to live by the English Heritage notice I don't know either.

The in-bye fields between Eastmoor and Bunker's Hill Wood, 1,000 feet above sea level, windswept and bleak in late winter, but a glorious walk in summer.

NORTH

There are three options when walking northwards from the House car park – the farm track below the Farmyard paddocks, the tarmac drive between the mile-long avenue of limes, or along the riverside.

THE BIG FLAT

If you choose the riverside, you will cross the Big Flat. This is where we hold the major park events – the Horse Trials, concerts (classical and pop) and the Country Fair. Many thousands of people come to all these entertainments, which give cheerful days and evenings and make a vital contribution to the upkeep of the place.

If people arrive by helicopter they have not far to walk but every step is hazardous for pale London shoes as a result of the 1,000 ewes that graze here and I notice much picking up of heels and craning round to see what damage has been done.

The Big Flat, which stretches out to the river north-west of the house, is a large enough site for the huge crowds that gather for the park events.

DRAINS

Most people walking in the park or across the fields will have no idea that they are treading on an intricate network of drains, joining one another like B roads and motorways. These were made by our ancestors and are now kept in order by the unusual talent of the Domain men.

Drains are a regular topic of conversation here. I am accustomed to hearing about them because my father was devoted to them and was chairman of the Drains Committee in the House of Lords for many years. Unluckily he never met Andrew's grandmother, Evelyn Duchess, who spoke about them constantly. Drains and illness went hand in hand for her, and when she got going on these twin subjects it was difficult to steer her on to something more cheery. In spite of having been brought up with drains, as it were, I have inherited neither my father's nor my

The Derwent Valley Water Scheme, March 1906. The cast-iron pipes made in Staveley are still there. A narrow-gauge railway was laid to bring them from Rowsley.

grandmother-in-law's head for them, and have little learning on the subject. I revere all the more those who have.

There is no map to show the precise routes of the channels, but the Domain men seem to carry divining rods in their heads and have an unerring instinct as to their whereabouts. When they sense trouble and start digging to find the offending drain, they do not dig in vain.

The pipes and drains come in all shapes and sizes. Some are hundreds of years old. The stone soughs are masterpieces of construction, built as the Romans built their water courses. A flat stone flag forms the base and two low stone walls make the sides. Massive flagstones bridge the top and complete the subterranean stream. Some are buried deep, but some are just beneath the sod and they are the ones that are easily broken and cause trouble.

When men, cows, sheep and horses and carts were the only traffic that these ancient structures had to bear, they did their job, out of sight and out of mind. Now heavy tractors, with wheels and cleated tyres higher than a man, and articulated lorries laden with beer and other consumer excitements for gatherings in the park, bring disaster to the system. They cause the stone flags to crack and the turf to become impacted; and so after rain the water lies on the impenetrable ground, making the place look miserable. Even the sheep, which do such a great job in levelling ruts with their 'golden hooves', could not face the canals and water jumps made by the wheels of the articulated lorries that got stuck and had to be dragged to and from the road by the JCB

While the work was going on to lay the pipes, the navvies slept inside them.

in the wet autumn of 1988, and the grass was scarred and made hideous for a long time.

Stone soughs are still the backbone of the drainage. They are very expensive to maintain, and to construct new ones would be out of the question. The rest of the skeleton is made up of untold miles of clay-pipe drains of all shapes and sizes. The ancient horseshoe type is shaped like an inverted U, each 'pipe' being about a foot long. They were laid in an open trench, sometimes on flat tiles and sometimes on a beaten earth or clay bottom. More modern, round-section clay pipes, which combine the ease of handling and relative cheapness of the horseshoe drain with an enclosed, and therefore stronger, circular shape, have been the mainstay of land drainage for many years. These pipes are now used for virtually all drains and can be made of clay, concrete, steel, fibreglass, plastic and other specialist materials as the job demands.

THE CRICKET PAVILION

The riverside route northwards takes you past the cricket ground and its pavilion, re-thatched in 2002 with reeds from Austria, of all the unlikely places. The annual match between my grandson William Burlington's XI and the Chatsworth XI is as keenly fought as those of years ago when the 9th Duke's agent advertised for an assistant who 'must be a good fast bowler' – an unusual postscript to a job description. The cricket club has a long tradition. It thrives and the fixture list is full. In 2003 Andrew suggested Chatsworth should have a ladies' eleven. This came about and gives much pleasure and a good deal of merriment to players and spectators alike.

The view from the pavilion is as good as any you could find. The belvedere crowning the north wing of the House rises above the trees and the white plume of the Emperor Fountain throws up 'its endless variety to the sky', as the 6th Duke described it.

BARBROOK HOUSE

The high wall of the old kitchen garden at Barbrook shelters the cricket ground from the north. In Paxton's time the 7 acres of once-productive ground were filled with extravagances including pineapple pits and experimental greenhouses of all kinds. His own imposing house was here too. All that remains is the garden's perimeter wall, the house's copper-roofed entrance lodge and some boulders, like those in the rock garden at Chatsworth.

Barbrook House was an 18th-century cottage when the 23-year-old Joseph Paxton arrived as head gardener in 1826 and he moved into it. Over the next twenty-five years it was progressively enlarged for him and his growing family and responsibilities. Offices were added, from which he eventually administered the estate, and it was here that he designed the Crystal Palace. The final additions to the house were built in the most exuberant and fanciful Victorian taste; one of the Crace family decorated the dining room in high Gothic style, and a grand conservatory was attached.

The entrance lodge, now known as the White Lodge, has a distinctive white-painted 'pelmet' under the roof like those on the shelters over platforms on railway stations. Paxton became a director of the railways and this is his oft-repeated and unforgettable signature.

Barbrook has changed its ways since the 1950s. The house, unoccupied since 1946, soon fell victim to dry rot. Pigs were kept on the ground floor, the dining room was a grain store and a few tons of potatoes were shovelled through the front door into the drawing room. In the 1950s the kitchen garden was finally abandoned; the glasshouses fell to pieces, sycamores invaded the roofless lily house and the whole area was desolate; Barbrook by now was in a parlous state.

BOTTOM Cricket has always been an important ingredient of English country village life and Chatsworth is no exception. The little thatched pavilion, sheltered from the north by tall trees and the old kitchen garden wall at Barbrook, has an idyllic feel about it on a summer's day.

The river is near enough for a mighty whack to send a ball into it.

TOP LEFT Chatsworth v. Bolton Abbey in 1935. The father of this book's photographer, Bridget Flemming née Wales, is fourth from the right, middle row.

TOP RIGHT William Burlington's XI v. Chatsworth Ladies, 2004. The Ladies won by seven wickets.

Barbrook House, which was enlarged over 25 years by Joseph Paxton for his own occupation from 1826. It was demolished in 1963.

At that time there seemed to be no future for such a big house. The outlook for Chatsworth itself was grim. The estate was crippled by the bill for death duties, and hundreds of cottages needed bathrooms and indoor lavatories. Barbrook was the sort of white elephant that the place could do without. It was demolished in 1963 and the hideous new Building Yard was completed on the site in 1966. It has changed its use again and is now a store, ready for any demands which may arise.

In what was Paxton's own garden are three 'log cabins', which were planned as worthy successors of the Russian Cottage but ended up as plain as can be, only just sliding through planning permission in 1973–4. They were an experiment in using home-grown timber. The builders thought they would not last more than about thirty years, but they are still happily lived in and enjoyed by their tenants. Signs of Paxton's occupancy are the rocks along the drive to the log houses.

It was difficult to know what to do with the old kitchen garden, a plot in the middle of the park, accessible only by a private road. Eventually it was decided to offer it to the Caravan Club, who took a thirty-year lease on the 7 acres within the wall and made a new approach from the A619 at Baslow. It opened in the late summer of 1987.

In 1989 we planted an avenue of beech and sycamore along the length of the track to make a drive between the quickthorn hedges of the Home Farm fields for the pleasure of our travelling guests who find a temporary home in the old garden.

The Caravan Club sets the highest possible standard of behaviour for its members, who are the most considerate paying guests imaginable, but for some reason they are wedded to vans of pale colours which are not objects of beauty. Here they are hidden by trees and the high kitchen-garden wall. A door was made in this wall, so that the visitors can walk straight into the park, and it is a real pleasure to see people enjoying the long, green summer evenings in these tranquil surroundings.

The short avenue that runs from the lodge to the main drive between Chatsworth and the Golden Gates is lined with red-twigged limes (*Tilia platyphyllos* 'Rubra') that we planted to mark the coronation of The Queen in 1953.

The White Lodge to Paxton's house. The white-painted wooden pelmet is a Paxton signature, repeated on many a station shelter.

BARBROOK TO BASLOW

A stone gatepost and an oak tree near the entrance to Barbrook and Home Farm, where he lived, are memorials to Jean-Pierre Béraud, the young Frenchman who did so much for Chatsworth in his eighteen years as chef in various departments. In 1996 he lost control of his new car, and it left the road and turned over, coming to rest here. His companion was unhurt but, to the sorrow of all who knew him, Jean-Pierre died: the end of an extraordinary career.

Going north you keep the Bar Brook on your left and see the 70 acres of flat fields of the Home Farm (called Crimea on some maps, indicating that the farm buildings were built around 1856) between that stream and the River Derwent. The massive stone wall running east–west dividing the first two fields was the boundary of the park till its enlargement in the 1830s.

Flooding of the Home Farm and the riverside houses in Baslow was a regular occurrence till the Bar Brook was deepened in 1974. In July 1973, after three days of torrential rain, the flood

The Bar Brook runs beside the footpath to the park from Goose Green in Baslow.

The Peacock Hotel, Baslow in *c.* 1900. It is now the Cavendish Hotel.

water was 3 feet deep in the farm buildings, and the telephone in the office floated off its table. If the Shetland ponies that I used to have had been in the yard, the bigger mares might have survived, but the foals would surely have drowned.

The only way out of the park for pedestrians is through the kissing gate (ingeniously designed to allow a wheelchair through) whence two paths lead to Baslow: one to Goose Green and the village hall and the other over a narrow stone footbridge across the Bar Brook to the Cavendish Hotel and a good lunch. Nailed to an alder tree on the bank is a notice with the sharp reminder 'Angling is not allowed in this Brook'.

BASLOW

Enlarging the Cavendish Hotel in Baslow is the biggest building job that has been done by the estate over the last twenty years. After Eric Marsh took on the tenancy in 1975, the hotel became so successful that he needed more bedrooms, so a new wing containing ten bedrooms and bathrooms was added. The first sod was cut on 19 September 1985 and the rooms were occupied by hotel guests six months later. The stone came from a knocked-down mill in Bradford and the building looks as if it has always been there – the highest praise you can give in this era of architectural stagnation.

PARK HOUSE

If you stay in the park, you can catch a glimpse of Park House, next to the Golden Gates lodges. A regulation, turreted, Italianate building, it was designed by Paxton's protégé John Robertson in 1842 for the 6th Duke's physician. A surgery with a separate entrance was provided. Dr Condell looked after the employees as well as the employer from 1837 to 1862. He was succeeded by Dr Wrench, who was the Baslow doctor for nearly fifty years.

Dr Wrench served in the Crimean War and witnessed the Indian Mutiny as a regimental medical officer before coming to Baslow to ply his trade under less hazardous conditions. The good doctor played a leading part in village life, and the little poplar wood in front of Park House is still called Wrench's Plantation.

His successor was Dr Edleston, who practised in Baslow from 1902 to 1938. Dr Sinclair Evans arrived in 1935 and retired in 1978, so Baslow knew only four doctors in 141 years.

In Dr Evans's early days as general practitioner Andrew's grandfather, Victor, was the 9th Duke. Dr Evans told me that until Victor died in 1938 the doctor who was called to the House at Chatsworth was expected to wear a dinner jacket if his visit was after 6.00 p.m. The rule held whether he was to see the Duke or the youngest kitchen maid.

GOLDEN GATES

You cannot fail to miss Chatsworth's grandest entrance. Framed by two lodges are the 1st Duke's gates, which were moved from the

Park House, very Paxtonian, was Dr Wrench's house. The surgery was stuck on.

West Terrace of the House and separated from their pair (which now forms the centre gate of the North Entrance) when the park was enlarged in the 1830s. They have been called the Sheffield, Baslow, Yorkshire or Turret Gates as well as the Golden Gates – five names for two gates. The last was a misnomer for years till 1988 when we beautified them by having Tijou's tracery in iron regilded. Jean Tijou was a French Hugenot who had worked for the King at Hampton Court Palace before coming to Chatsworth. Twice I have known them to be bashed by runaway lorries, and the delicate ironwork, including the lacy urns that crown them, has been mended to look as good as new. The skill of the smith survives.

BASLOW LODGES

The lodges flanking the Golden Gates were the last of Sir Jeffry Wyatville's grand designs for his patron, the Bachelor Duke. They were built in 1839–42, and completed after the architect died. Decimus Burton was responsible for the stone piers. The 17th-century ironwork and the 19th-century wall and lodges are a typical Chatsworth jumble of dates and designers, successfully joined together for use and beauty.

The belt of trees that screens the A619 to Chesterfield was planted after the enlargement of the park in the 1830s. It is called Heathy Lea, and the very old house of the same name sits like a broody hen overlooking her end of the park. The wood above the house is Jumble Coppice.

JUBILEE ROCK AND DOBB EDGE

Returning to the House by walking south across the hill you will find the Jubilee Rock, or Elephant Rock as the solitary lump of millstone grit used to be called. Its shape, grey colour and surface of folds are strangely like the loose skin of an elephant. Dr Wrench, staunchly royalist, had an inscription carved on it to mark the Golden Jubilee of Queen Victoria in 1887, and he organised a jolly party for the village for the unveiling of his loyal message on the rock.

Tijou's gates of 1692–3 were moved here in the 1830s. Their pair is at the entrance to the North Front of the House.

The massive Jubilee Rock at the north end of the park.

Further south from the Jubilee Rock you leave a few acres of ancient scrub oak and bracken on the hill to your left, Dobb Edge, a favourite gathering ground of the fallow deer. A small area was fenced in 1995 in the hope of the oaks regenerating. They stubbornly refuse to do so. Some unfinished millstones lie where they were quarried from the rocks. A badger lived in a drain near here, and my old collie dog used to get very agitated at the first whiff.

South of the footpath from Baslow to Stand Wood is Brickhill Pond, home of the great crested newt. If you can find one (which I doubt) don't touch it, or you'll go to prison: it is a protected species. This is where the clay came from which made the bricks for the old kitchen-garden wall and other buildings.

THE ICE HOUSE AND POND

Next comes the Ice House and the scooped-out flat ground on which the water could be made to flood so that it might freeze. There was an ice house at Chatsworth as early as 1693 but its exact location is not known. This one under the bank dates from the mid-18th century and is brick-lined. The ice was cut into blocks and stored in it for summer use. This was done every winter till the 1920s, when the first refrigerators were bought for the kitchen, to the delight of the cook, who did not appreciate the 'swan's dirt' and other bits and pieces present in natural ice.

TERCENTENARY AVENUE

The year 1994 marked the tercentenary of the dukedom – the three hundredth anniversary of William of Orange's reward to the Earl of Devonshire for his part in bringing him to the throne of England. After much thought and visits to the wonderful lime avenue in Clumber Park, Nottinghamshire, and others we decided to celebrate this historic date by planting a lime avenue from the Golden Gates to below the Rookery Wood.

The Domain men, led by David Robinson, measured the distance of 22 yards apart for the 153 cloned Kaiser Linden trees (*Tilia* x *europaea* 'Pallida'), which came from Holland. There are 75 on each side of the road plus 3 on the triangle at the south end. The holes were dug and tree guards put up – a major task

Dobb Edge. The Millennium Stone was brought to The Crobs from here.

which included inserting a pipe through which to water the young trees in case of drought.

The most northerly pair were planted by The Prince of Wales and Senator Edward Kennedy, who happened to be with us on the same day. The young trees are thriving and will soon turn into an important feature of the drive to the Golden Gates.

THE E II R WALL

In 2002 the question of how to celebrate the Queen's Golden Jubilee arose: another planting of trees to echo those on the steep slope of Bramley Dale, perhaps? There the letters E R are beeches against a background of evergreens, generally thought to be a successful eye-catcher for her loyal subjects. It was Geoff Machin, head forester, who suggested a stone wall (or walls, as they turned out to be) of the local Derbyshire material, weather-proof, long-lasting and built by the skilled men who are responsible for the many miles of walling in the Peak District.

Everyone liked the idea. The hill above the old rifle butts in the field of that name, an east-facing bank over the river which is seen from a private road in the park, always open to walkers but not cars, seemed a perfect site. Two hundred and fifty tonnes of

LEFT The almost invisible Ice House, built underground of brick with a domed roof.

OPPOSITE The E II R Wall, constructed in honour of the Golden Jubilee of HM The Queen by stone wallers who volunteered to do the job. The letters and figures are 30 inches (0.75m) high.

Pegasus by Tim Harrisson, 2002.

Two Column Jump by David Nash, 2003.

reclaimed gritstone were shifted to the site by estate staff. The cipher 'E II R' was marked out by 765 yards (700 metres) of string and 312 yards (285 linear metres) of walling was built 30 inches (0.75 metres) high. From 19 to 24 May twenty dry stone wallers and helpers, mostly volunteers, worked for 1,300 hours to build this historic document to honour Her Majesty.

Their creation is seen and admired by all who use the north drive to Baslow and the Golden Gates.

THE HORSE TRIAL FENCES

The cross-country course, a phase of the Horse Trials that are an annual spring event at Chatsworth, spreads across part of the Big Flat and above and beyond the Ice House. Every year a sculptor, commissioned by Sto and Amanda, makes a permanent, testing fence for the competitors. The position, materials and scale of each fence is agreed between the artist and the course designer so that it becomes a safe, effective and exciting addition to the course.

So far we have examples of the work of Alison Crowther, Allen Jones, Tim Harrisson, David Nash and Nigel Ross. They are not only a unique part of the competition, but also add great interest to a walk round the park – an out-of-doors extension of the sculpture gallery in the House for all to enjoy.

RIGHT clockwise, from top left: T*he Two Graces* by Allen Jones, 2000, *The Lover's Seat* by Alison Crowther, 1999, and *Epona's Leap* by Nigel Ross, 2005.

THE CHATSWORTH SETTLEMENT and the CHATSWORTH HOUSE TRUST

In 1980, at the request of Andrew and our son Peregrine (Stoker) Hartington, the Trustees of the Chatsworth Settlement granted a 99-year lease at a rent of £1 per annum of Chatsworth House, its essential contents, garden, park and some woods, a total of 1,569 acres (to which an additional 253 acres of woodland were added in 1994) to a charitable foundation called Chatsworth House Trust. The object of the Trust is the 'long-term preservation of Chatsworth for the benefit of the public'. A capital sum was raised by the sale of works of art from the private side of the House and from other family resources. The income from this trust fund goes towards the upkeep of the House, garden and park, which are now the responsibility of the Council of Management of Chatsworth House Trust. The family is represented on the Council, but there is a majority of independent members. Andrew and his Trustees never applied for a government grant for restoration of the Grade I Listed buildings leased to the House Trust. These buildings are maintained exclusively from the resources of the House Trust, the income from visitors and 10 per cent of the turnover of the Orangery and Carriage House shops and restaurant.

Peculiar local windows: all different and a glazier's education. They can be seen in Edensor, at the Hunting Tower and at Redway Farm.

INDEX

Page numbers in *italic* refer to captions to the illustrations

Going back inside through the West Front door.

AUTHOR'S ACKNOWLEDGEMENTS

This is really Bridget Flemming's book. Her photographs impelled me to do the written part.

I would like to thank the following Chatsworth people for their invaluable help: Stuart Band, Archivist; Julie Davison, Personnel; Sean Doxey, Clerk of Works; Ian Else, Surveyor; John Hill, retired Tractor Driver; Robert Hill, Accountant; Geoff Machin, Head Forester; Charles Noble, Collection; Margaret Norris, Farmyard & Adventure Playground Manager; Iain Nott, Assistant Agent; John Oliver, Comptroller; Derrick Penrose, retired Agent; Andrew Peppitt, Archivist; David Robinson, Domain; Ian Turner, Farms Manager; Roger Wardle, Agent.

Brian Gilbert, Ian Fraser Martin, Diane Naylor and Robert Ollerenshaw kindly provided additional photographs.

Also, I am grateful for vital information from: Len Broome, retired tenant farmer; Ann Hall, Headteacher, Pilsley Church of England Primary School; Trevor Wragg, President, Derbyshire Dry Stone Walling Association.

My thanks to Tristram Holland, editor – clever, strict and kind.

Without Helen Marchant's help there would be no book.

D.D.

PUBLISHER'S ACKNOWLEDGEMENTS
All photographs by Bridget Flemming except those on pages 69 right and 109 top right. All historic material by courtesy of the Trustees of the Chatsworth Settlement. Map illustration by Joanna Logan. Book design by Becky Clarke. Book production by Kim Oliver. Index by Marie Lorimer.

An old shearing shed, Edensor Lane.